www.ingramcontent.com/pod-product-compliance
Ingram Content Group UK Ltd.
Pitfield, Milton Keynes, MK11 3LW, UK
UKHW021336280125
4330UKWH00006B/549

FAIRBAIRN'S CRESTS OF THE FAMILIES OF Great Britain and Ireland.

Compiled From the best Authorities by James Fairbairn.

AND REVISED BY

LAURENCE BUTTERS,

Seal Engraver in ordinary to the Queen for Scotland

EDITED BY JOSEPH MACLAREN

VOLUME SECOND

EDINBURGH, THOMAS C. JACK, 92 PRINCES STREET

LONDON, HAMILTON, ADAMS & Co.

CONTENTS OF VOL. II.

PLATE 1.

PLATE 2.

James Fairbairn S. Edin'

PLATE 3.

James Fairbairn Sc Edin^r

PLATE 4.

PLATE 5.

Isaac Fairbairn Sc Edin

PLATE B.

PLATE 7.

PLATE B.

PLATE 9.

PLATE 10.

PLATE 11

PLATE 12.

PLATE 13.

PLATE 14.

PLATE 15.

PLATE 16.

PLATE 17.

PLATE 18.

James Fairbairn Sc. Edin[r]

PLATE 19.

PLATE 20.

PLATE 21.

PLATE 22.

PLATE 23.

PLATE 24.

James Fairbairn & C° Edin^r

PLATE 25.

PLATE 26.

PLATE 27.

PLATE 28.

PLATE 29.

PLATE 30.

PLATE 31

PLATE 32.

PLATE 33.

PLATE 34.

PLATE 35.

PLATE 38.

PLATE 37.

James Fairbairn Sc. Edin.

PLATE 36.

PLATE 39.

James Fairbairn Sc Edin[r]

PLATE 40.

PLATE 41.

James Fairbairn & Sons

PLATE 42.

PLATE 43.

[illegible]

PLATE 44.

PLATE 45.

PLATE 46.

James Fairburn Sc Edin

PLATE 47.

James Fairbairn & C° Edin.r

PLATE 48.

James Fairbairn Sc Edinr

PLATE 49.

James Fairbairn Sc Edinr

PLATE 50.

James Fairbairn, Sc Edin^{r}

PLATE 51.

James Fairbairn [illegible]

PLATE 52.

James Fairbairn Sc Edin^r

PLATE 53.

James Fairbairn Sc. Edin^r

PLATE 54.

PLATE 55.

PLATE 5B

James Fairbairn, Sc. Edin.

PLATE 57.

PLATE 58.

James Fairbairn Sc Edin[r]

PLATE 59.

James Fairbairn Sc. Edinr

PLATE 60.

PLATE 61.

PLATE 82.

PLATE 63.

PLATE 64.

1

2

3

4

5

6

7

8

9

10

11

12

13

14

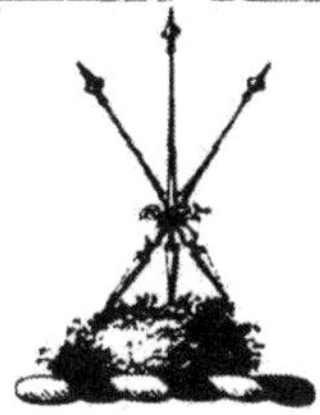
15

James [illegible] Co Edin[illegible]

PLATE 65.

PLATE 66.

PLATE 67.

PLATE 68.

James Fairbairn Sc. Edinr

PLATE 69.

PLATE 10.

PLATE 71.

[illegible]

PLATE 72.

James Fairbairn Sc Edin.

PLATE 73.

James Fairbairn, Co. Edinr

PLATE 74

James Fairbairn Sc. Edin.

PLATE 75.

PLATE 76.

James Fairbairn Sc Edin.r

PLATE 73.

James Fairbairn, Sc. Edin.

PLATE 78.

James Fairbairn Sc Edinr

PLATE 79.

James Fairbairn Sc. Edin.

PLATE 80.

James Fairbairn Sc. Edinr

PLATE 81.

James Fairbairn Sc. Edin.r

PLATE 82.

James Fairbairn Sc Edin.r

PLATE 83.

1

2

3

4

5

6

7

8

9

10

11

12

13

14

15

James Fairbairn Sc. Edin[r]

PLATE 84.

1

2

3

4

5

6

7

8

9

10

11

12

13

14

15

PLATE 85.

James Fairbairn & Edin.

PLATE 66.

James Fairbairn Sc. Edin.

PLATE 87

PLATE 88.

PLATE 8D.

PLATE 90.

James Fairbairn Sc. Edin[r]

PLATE 91.

James Fairbairn Sc Edin'

PLATE 92.

James Fairbairn Sc. Edinr

PLATE 93.

James Fairbairn, Sc. Edin^r

PLATE 94

PLATE 95.

PLATE 96.

PLATE 97.

PLATE 98.

PLATE 99

PLATE 100.

PLATE 101.

PLATE 102.

PLATE 103

PLATE 104.

PLATE 105.

James Fairbairn Sc. Edin.

PLATE 108.

PLATE 107.

[illegible]

PLATE 108.

1 2 3 4 5 6 7 8 9 10 11 12 13 14 15

PLATE 109.

James Fairbairn, Sc. Edin.

PLATE 110.

James Fairbairn Sc. Edin.

PLATE III.

PLATE 112.

James Fairbairn Jr. Edin[r]

PLATE 113.

PLATE 114.

PLATE 113.

PLATE 116.

PLATE 117.

James Fairbairn Sc Edin.

PLATE 11 B.

James Fairbairn Sc Edin[r]

PLATE 119.

PLATE 120.

PLATE 121.

James Fairbairn Sc Edin^r

PLATE 122.

PLATE 123.

James Fairbairn Sc. Edin.

PLATE 124.

PLATE 125.

PLATE 126.

James Fairbairn Jr Sculpt

PLATE 126*a*

James Fairbairn Sc. Edin^r

PLATE 126*b*.

PLATE 126.

PLATE 126d.

PLATE 127.

James Fairbairn Sc. Edin.

PLATE 128.

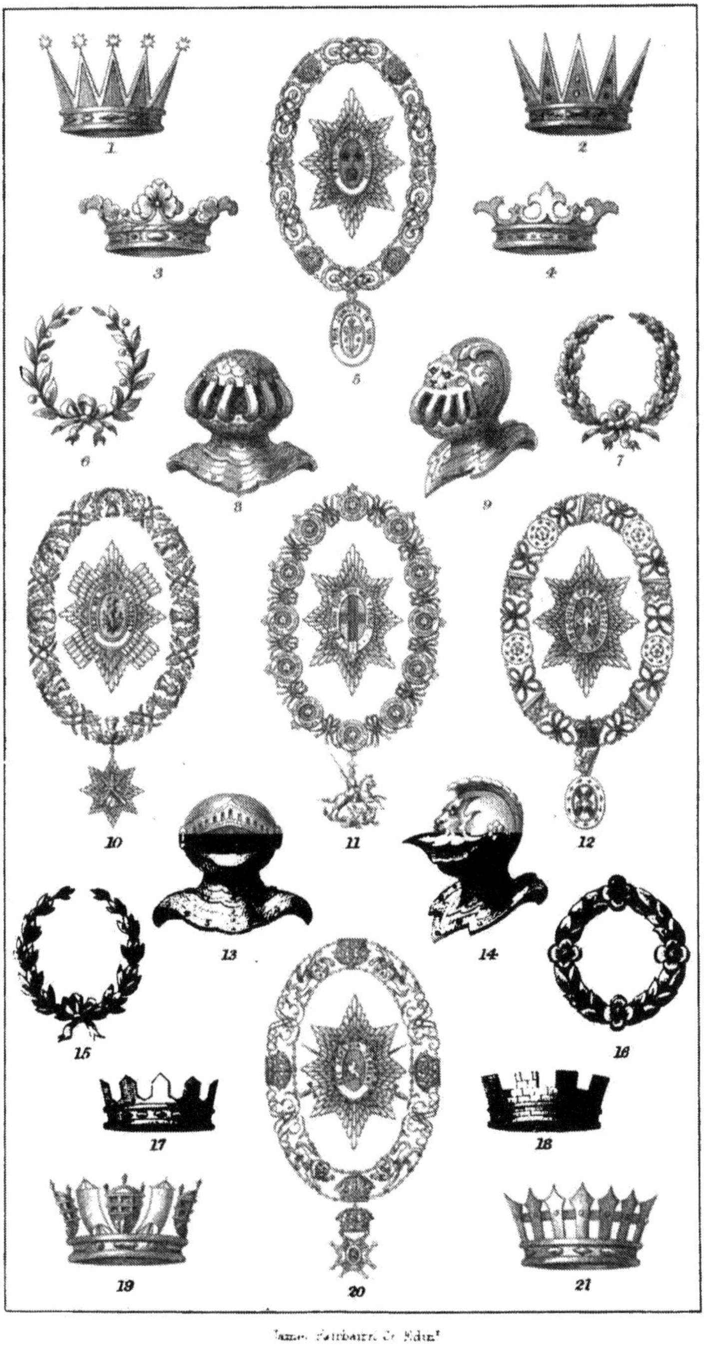

James Fairbairn & Co. Edin.

PLATE 129.

1
2
3
4
5
6
7
8
9
10
11
12
13
14
15
16
17
18
19
20
21
22
23
Gold
Silver
Red
Blue
Black
Green
Purple

PLATE 13D.

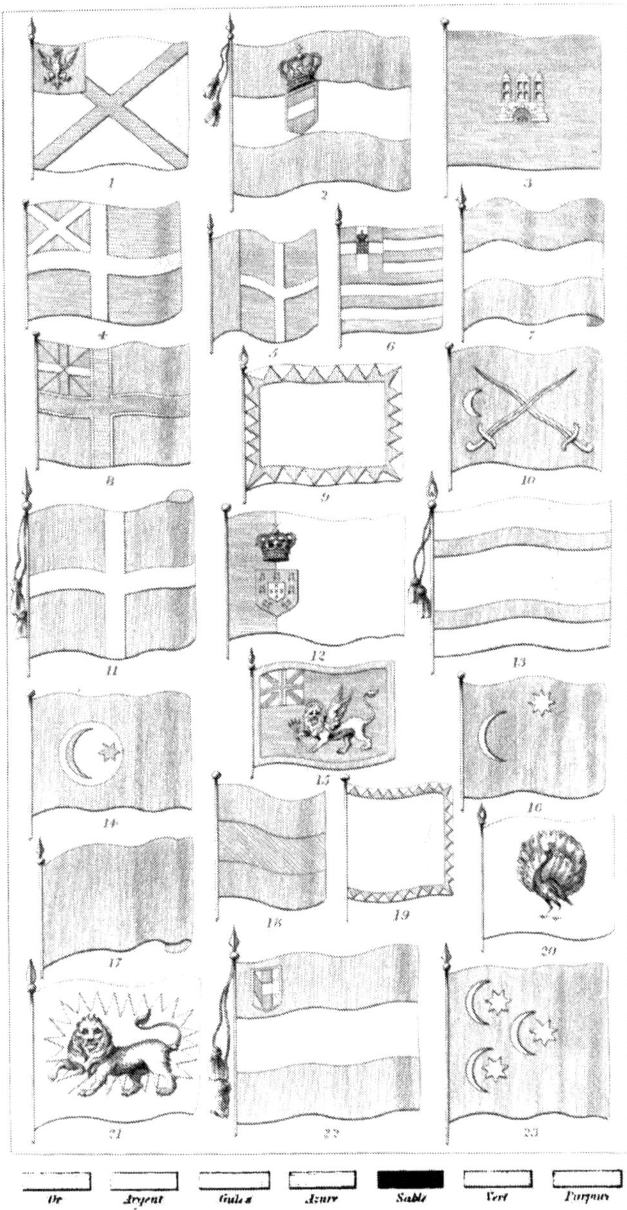

PLATE 131.

PLATE 132.

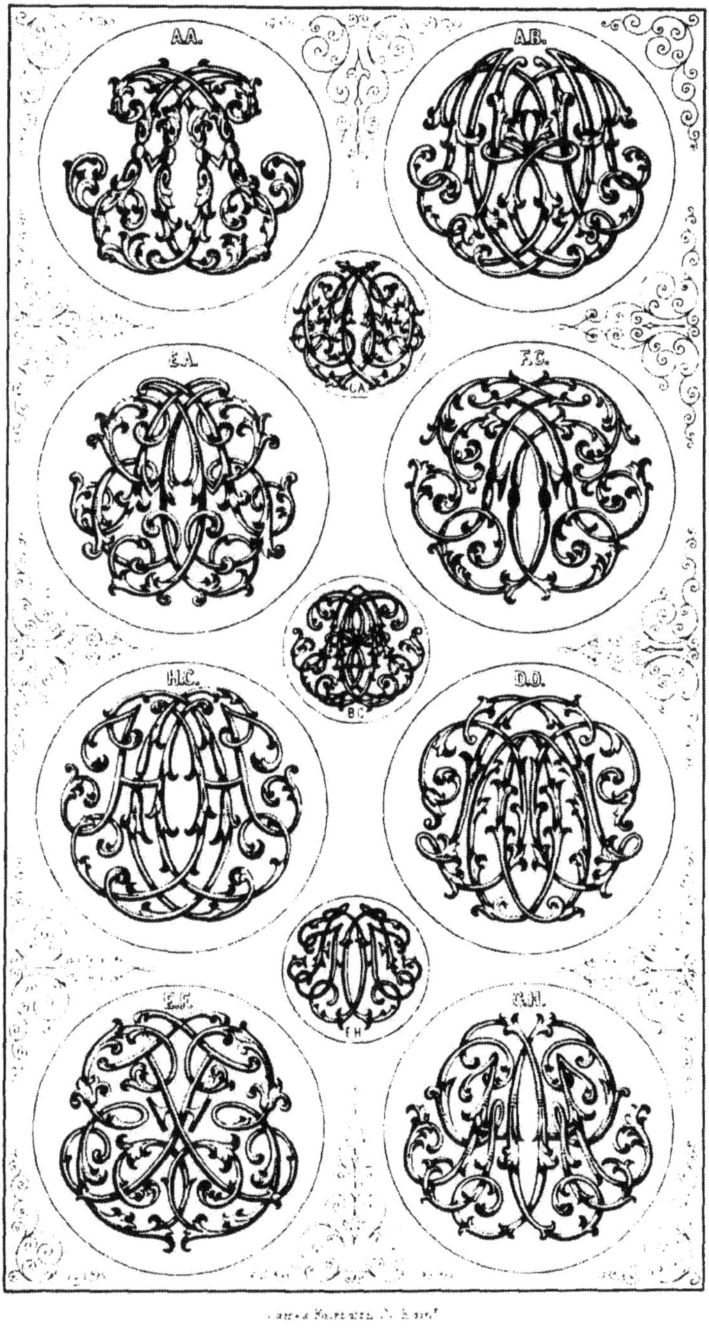

PLATE 133.

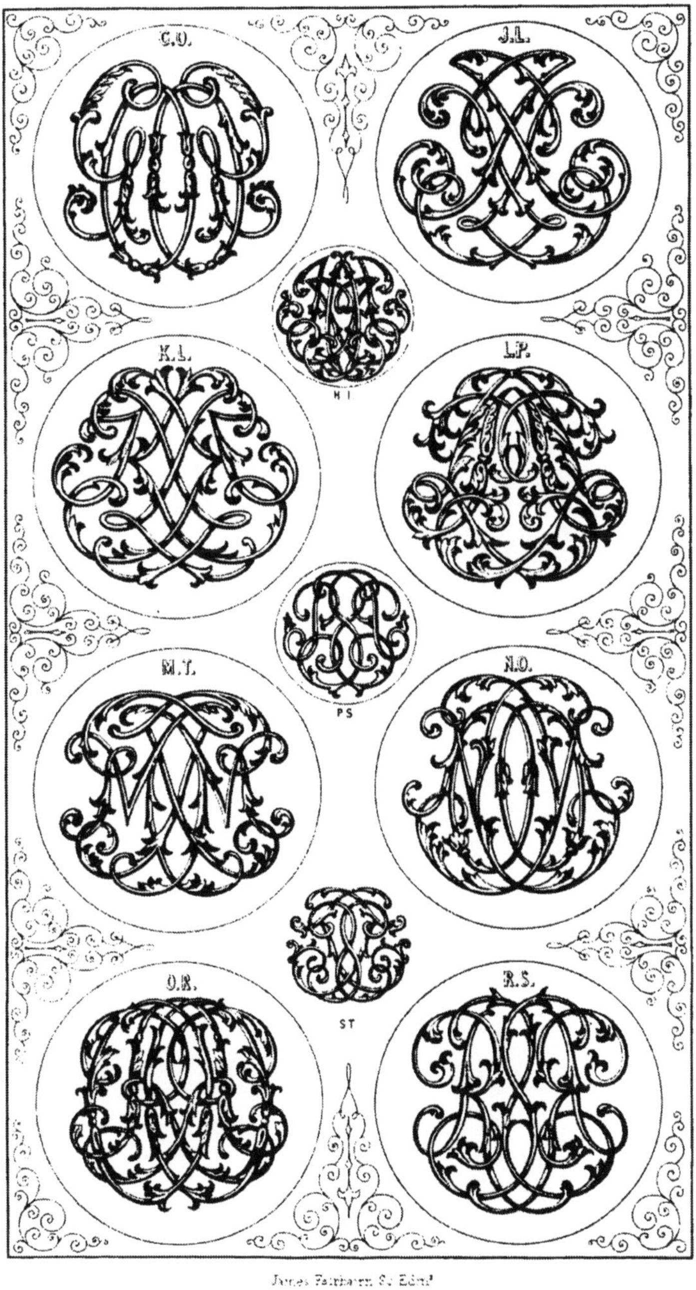

James Fairbairn Sc Edin^r

PLATE 134.

James Fairbairn C° Edin^r

PLATE 155.

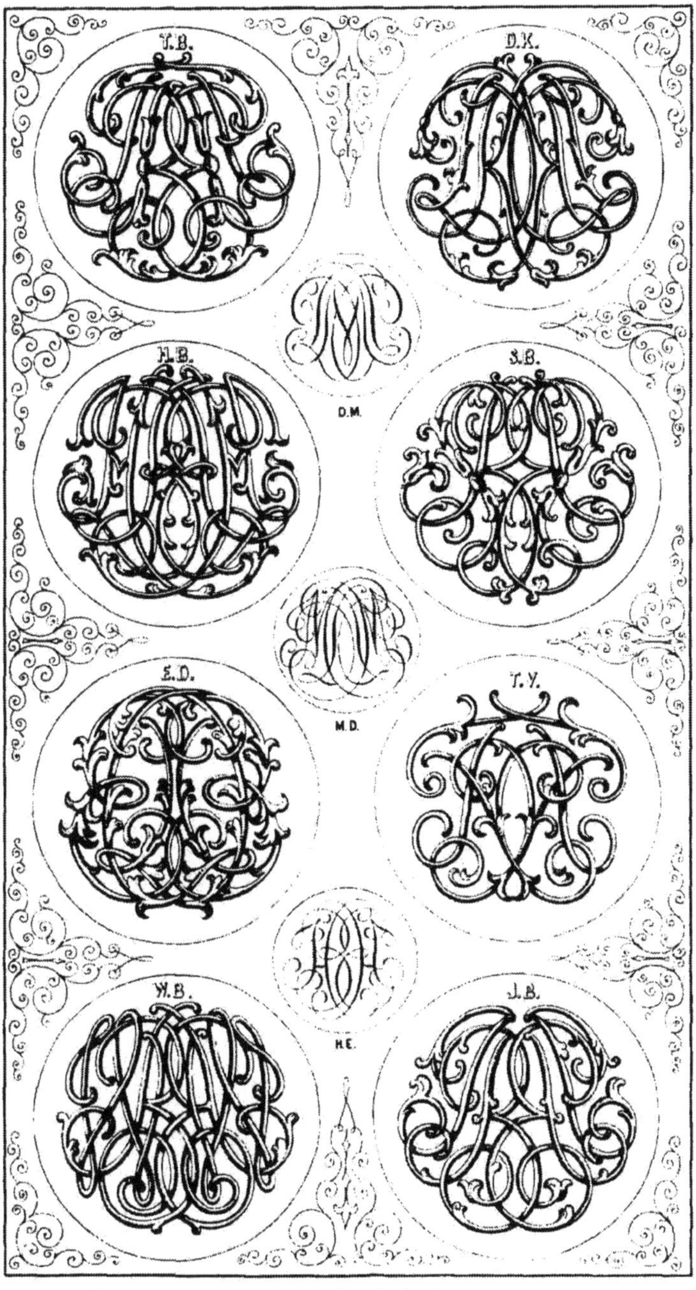

PLATE 136.

PLATE 137.

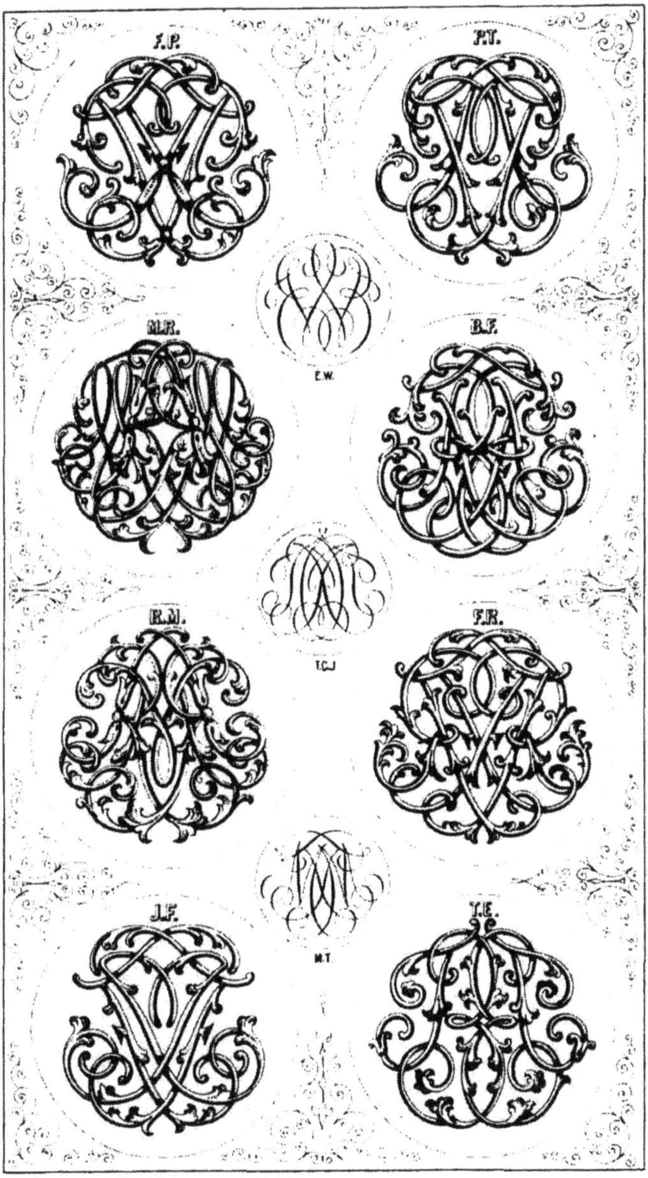

James Fairbairn Sc. Edinr

PLATE 138.

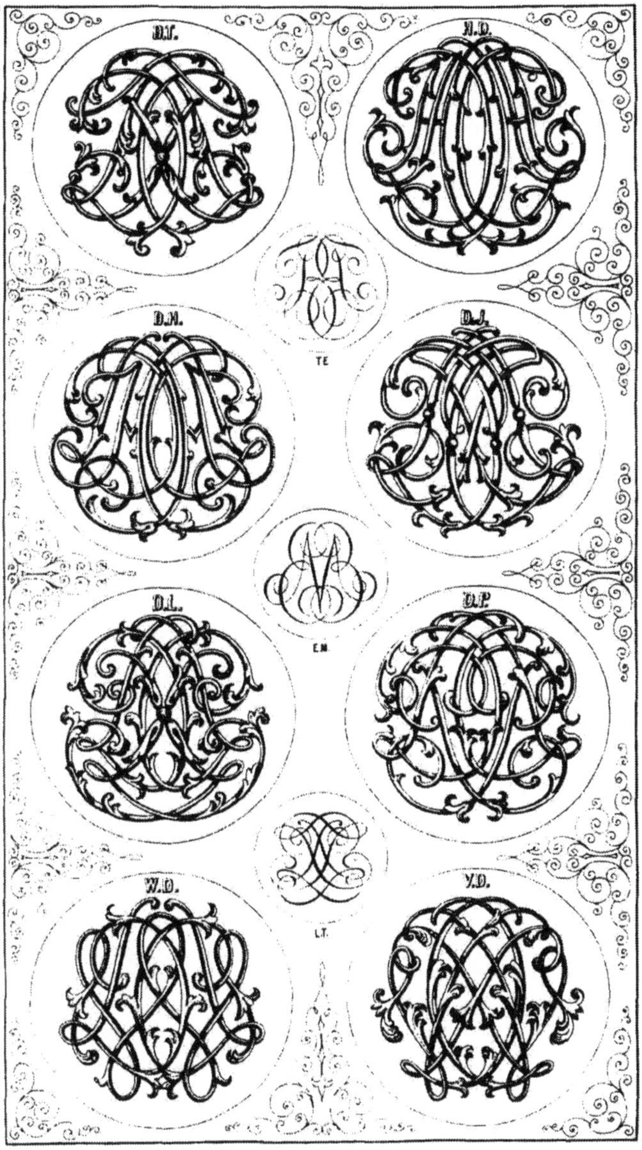

James Fairbairn Jr. Engd

PLATE 139.

James Fairbairn Sc Edin.

PLATE 140.

PLATE 141.

James Fairbairn Sc. Edin^r

PLATE 142.

PLATE 143.

DIRIGE
NOS
London
CONCILIO ET LABORE
Manchester
BON ACCORD
Aberdeen

PLATE 144.

Edinburgh

Regalia of Scotland

Birmingham

Sheffield

KEY TO CREST PLATES.

PLATE 1.

CREST

1. Alexander, Mee, Stormyn.
2. Alexander, Buchanan, Haulton, Hurot, Lestrange, Liston, Miller, Strange, Straunge, Wayland.
3. Alges, Algie, Algoe, Gwynne, Lyte, Moone, Sidney.
4. Baxter, Budgen, Hounhill, Hownhill, Majoribanks, Marjoribanks, Rothings, Wardell.
5. Badd, Baud, Baude, Castilion, Wright, Wroth, Wrothe.
6. Bateson, Batson, Harvey-Bateson.
7. Bowlby, Bracken, Byres, Cauty, Dowding, Fitz-Marmaduke, Lax, Mawgyron, Pitman.
8. Calverlye, Catt, Catton, Esmond, Gottington, Harbin, Jennoway, Massie, Rumsey.
9. Candlish, Cavendish, Fleming, Honnor, Honor, Huxley, Lante, M'Candlish, Mathilez, Melton, Pringle, Simpson, Southern.
10. Delancey, Delancy, De Lancey.
11. Boreman, Cockfield, Cokefield, De Hatfield, Grafton, Hatfield, Man.
12. Capper, Chester, Cousen, Cremer, Cupholme, De Dreux, Delavall, Dusseaux, Grigson, Huson, Martineau, Newnham, Penruddock, Penruddocke, Sackvill, Swayne, Sydenham, Weaver.
13. Bott, Cleland-Rose, Eresey, Gonne, Jenney, Jobson, Leech, Leeche, Strutt.
14. Estday, Hawkins.
15. Ashburton, Audeley, Baring, Duntze, Evershead, Greenwood, Kilgour, Muilman.

PLATE 2.

1. Acheson, Aitchison, Atcheson, Blackburn, Blackburne, Gosford, Lever, Sinclair.
2. Ackerman, Ackermann, Acraman, Akerman, Cordingley, Lasman, Symeon.
3. Acton, Allardas, Allardes, Allardice, Allerdes, Allerdyce, Bayne, Beaghan, Gambon, Gamon, Jameson, Jamieson, Kers, Mortimer, Nordet.
4. Baldwin, Cartaret, Feilden, Garnatt, Holt, Percy-Fielding.
5. Balfour.
6. Ball, Gillon, Greenland, Hallom, Handfield, Purling, Scobell, Sommerville, Wastoile, Wastoyle.
7. Badeley, Brackesby, Brigham, Brookesby, Burwood, Calthorp, Calthorpe, Calthrop, Eychebald, Galbraith, Gordon, Greig, Harvie, Home, Hubbert, Kirke, Loveland, Lowe, Tetley, Vair, Wardall.
8. Able, Aldworth, Alexander, Areskine, Armstrong, Ashtown, Athill, Athyll, Bagley, Bellew, Brace, Breanon, Brouncker, Brownlee, Brownlie, Butler, Cameron, Carnell, Carvile, Chepstow, Chevil, Claydan, Clifton, Conner, Connour, Conyngham, Cruikshank, Cunninghame, Curtis, Delarous, Donald, Dowglas, Ellicombe, Engleheart, Enson, Erskine, Freke, Fry, Gissing, Gissinge, Gledstanes, Goadefroy, Goodhand, Grant, Gun, Guthrie, Hacket, Harvey, Jack, John, Kane, Keir, Laugton, Laungton, Litchfield, Lutwich, Lutwyche, M'Beath, M'Donald, MacMahon, M'Vean, Maguire, Mansfield, Mathew, Mathews, Merriman, Mirehouse, Mounsey, Neal, Neale-Burrard, Newborough, Newby, Newport, O'Breanon, O'Connor, Odel, O'Learie, Ory, Pace, Paulet, Phillpotts, Pollett, Pomfree, Porter, Poulett, Probert, Quin, Rawle, Rawlins, Rokeston, Ross, Rule, Salmon, Serres, Simcoe, Smith, Smyth, Spange, Stratford, Taafe, Toulmin, Trench, Vane, Wade, Wall, Wallace, Warham, Warrand, White, Wolston, Wolstone, Wyrrall.
9. Ashley, Brereton, Brewerton, Campion, Campyon, Craddock, Cradock, Forbes, Forbs, Galbraith, Groyn, Hasard, Joseline, Josselin, Josselyne, Laing, Lascelles, Lascells, Lassells, Laslett, Rawlins, Whittle.
10. Darcey, D'Arcy, Ogilvie.
11. Boston, Cam, Camm, Dove, Miles, Pytts, Swinton, Swynton, Torrings.
12. Cupples, Delamaine, Dryland, Pitcher, Ratford, Seton.
13. Edge.
14. Edmondson.
15. Aldham, Alexander, Allen, Barritt, Blood, Conarton, Cotterell, Duncombe, Egleston, Eyer, Fenn, Fisher, Flamsted, Forster, Foster-Hill, Hadokes, Hall, Haswell, Kiddell, King, Kinge, Lodge, M'Cay, M'Coy, Maxey, Maxie, Melvile, Myggs, Mylbourne, Parker, Phelps, Wallis, Watt, Whetteel, Whittell.

PLATE 3.

1. De la Vach, Delavache.
2. De Mandevile, M'Cabe, Partrickson, Patrickson, Shepard, Sheppard.
3. Ennys.
4. Borough, Fitz-Ronard.
5. Buchanan, Cartlitch, Depden, Fitz-Symon, Greetham, Lizurs, M'Kenzie, MacMillan, Murehead.
6. Borelands, Borland, Borlands, Cuiler, Ethelstan, Ethelston, Foskett, Tidmarsh.
7. Tolhalth.
8. Allen, Bunton, Dobree, Drummond, Drummond-Burrell, Gross, Kyllingbeck
9. Bloye, Jaffray, Marchall, Richmond, St. Leger, Vowell.
10. Colwick, Colwyke, Hazard, Newenham, Newmarch, Young.
11. Beriffe, Cooke.'
12. Colley, Grensby, Grymsby, Macklow, Nicolls.
13. Caltoft, Collinson, Green, Horton, Vigne.
14. Jones, Thorpe.
15. Collis.

PLATE 4.

1. Edgell, Edghill.
2. East.
3. Fairn.
4. Brook, Brooke, Falkiner, Faulkner.
5. Easum, Eston.
6. Aisincourt, Garbet.
7. Hackford, Leach, Shaw, Spooks, Tatham.
8. Faithfull.
9. Gardiner.
10. Hackwell, Hakewill, Van-Hagen.
11. Bigg, Gardiner, Pagrave, Wade, Wither-Bigg.
12. Haddon.
13. Ince.
14. Garratt, Garret, Garrett, Jarrett.
15. Irwin, Irwine.

PLATE 5.

1. Dunster.
2. Arkinstall, Beauchamp, Braithwait.
3. Parker.
4. Parker.
5. Newton, Parnell, Pownall.
6. Samwell.
7. Ralph, Rutson.
8. Randall.
9. Redman.
10. Thelusson.
11. Rankine.
12. Reynardson.
13. Reynolds.
14. Rattray.
15. Rixon, Walsingham.

PLATE 6.

1. Clements, Coyle, Gregor, Hawkes, Innes, Pery, Ragon, Riddock, Troup, Tyler, Underwood, Whitbread, Whitbred, Wooley.
2. Raban.
3. Moore, Radcliff-Delme.
4. Bartlett, St. Hill.
5. Delancey, Sabbe.
6. Berreton, Brereton, Gauntlet, Parker, St. Michael, St. Michell, Vincent, White.
7. Atteloùnde, Hamerton, Polleyne.
8. Tallantire.
9. Tash.
10. Utber, Utker.
11. Corrance, Urren.
12. Cheyney, Pede, Uvedale.
13. Beaumont, Cherveaux, Van.
14. Vachell.
15. Vandyk, Vandyke.

PLATE 7.

1. Ackland.
2. Acre, Akenside, Aker, Crawley, Cropper, Fulherst, Fulsherst, Johnson, M'Cullock, Porter.
3. Adair, Norman.
4. Ball, Garter, Miller, Pratt, Rampston, Rempston.
5. Balfour, Budd, Fletewood, Jacob, Osborn, Osborne, Skerret, Skull, Walrond.
6. Addworth, Agrevell, Agworth, Alde, Anna, Banister, Barns, Beechey, Beechy, Burn, Burne, Edward, Engolisme, Spelman, Udward.
7. Asborne, Ashborne, Ashbury, Auchterlony, Cameron, Cust, Moody.
8. Loudon.
9. Campbell, M'Gibbon, Steer.
10. Archbold, Archebold, Barr, Betenson, Bettenson, Betterson, Bettinson, Bettison, Bragg, Cator, Currer, Danncey, Dansey, Dauncey, Drew, Elven, Foster, Foulkes, Glynn, Gowans, Gunthorpe, Home, Hume, Huninges, Hunt, Kent, Kent-Egleton, Lapthorne, Lobb, Mawson, Morar, North, Oliver, Penrose, Pentland, Posynworth, Powell, Repley, Sutton, Trotter, Wendey, White.
11. Ahrends, Band, Bure, Carrington, Chappeace, Cosyn, Dapiper, Devenshire, Gwillanne, Jackson, Jervis-White, Lynedoch, Monro, Munro, Murray, Osmond, Reynold, Rutter, Tripp, Woolley.
12. Blaney, Blayney, Boston, Coulthart, Dally, Darley, Dick, Horsey, Maleverer.

PLATE 7—*continued.*

13. Carry, Coffin, Devendale, Egan, Fokeram, Gordon, Lapsley, Lapslie, Mackeill, Seagrim.
14. Edmund, Healey, Healy.
15. Arnaway, Arneway, Arnold, Arnway, Bischoff, Delapool, Delapoole, De la Poole, Edwards, Huntingdon, Huntington, Sherley, Sumner.

PLATE 8.

1. De Breteville, Dobbins, Dobins, Lovegrove, Loveplace.
2. Amosley, Bagenholt, Bolton, Boltone, Boltoun, Boulton, Bretrook, Dear, Deare, Gorman, Grosvenor.
3. De Clare, Deyncourt, Haselerton, Jasper, Kinarby, Sandell.
4. Candishe, Cavendish, Gant, Garnon, Gaunt, Gernon, Goodson, Lowe, Rowley, Style, Wood.
5. Aylemer, Aylener, Aylmer, Bunnell, Dellyne, Ithell, Rochefort.
6. Cosgrave, Finlayson, Goddard, Hutchon, Justine, Justyne, Ketford, Lewis, Quelch.
7. Alberough, Albrough, Nisbet.
8. Alberton, Hatch, Lennos, Lenos, Oray, Oyry, Todd.
9. Alabaster, Albaster, Allebaster, Arblaster, Burrowes, Burrows, Hatfield, Hitfield, Reye, Rye, Tudway.
10. Baron, English, Malcom, Malcolm.
11. Barkham, Dabernon, Debenham, Flowerdew, Flowerdue, Gover, Quarton.
12. Barrett, Chemere, Lawful, Montresor, Pecke, Shairp, Sharp.
13. Allmack Almack, Arnett, Arnot, Arnott, Awmack, Both, Bothe, Castlyn, Duckensfield, M'Callum.
14. Cathery, Scott.
15. Bridges, Casson, Dove, Levall.

PLATE 9.

1. Jejeebhoy.
2. Pittillo.
3. Wallace.
4. Berkenhead, Boland, Cranber, Dennis, Hassall, Hassell, Hatch, Parnell.
5. Blayney, Bygan, Chawner, Crawford, Ermine, Jaye, Keith, Lewis, M'Culloch, Robe, Stanton, White.
6. Babington, Barker, Bowdon, Channy, Charnell, Cornish, Cotton, Cressy, Delves, Fownes, Francis, Gent, Graby, Greby, Graves, Jenningham, Johnson, Kensington, Meadows, Medlycott, Pakenham, Parkins, Pring, Prinne, Quarles, Rodney, Scarlett, Scroy, Skory, Slater, Stoner, Warrington, Webb, Webbe-Weston, White.
7. Beseley, Besley, Bealy, Craddock, Cradock, Ford, Roper.
8. Berwick, Cundall, Cundill, Cundy, Handford, Lindsay, Lynch.
9. Aprece, Barrie, Bethune, Bradwarden, St. Germyn, Sinclair, Tayler.
10. Clendon, Giberne, Haney, Murray, Power.
11. Champneis, Champneys, Durward, Lee.
12. Channsy, Chansey, Chase, Hillaire, Keay, Key.
13. Cherley.
14. Anderson, Atye, Attye, Senior.
15. Cheney, Cheyney, Crownall, Dalrymple, Horn, Morrell, Sherland, Sulby.

PLATE 10.

1. Hacker, Halifad.
2. Chitwynde, Hake.
3. Halberdyn, Watkins.
4. Inys.
5. Halford.
6. Ireys.
7. Jackerell.
8. Irving.
9. Jary.
10. Dallas, Keddie.
11. Kadie.
12. Charnock, Eccleston, Eclestone, Goldfinch, Goodbridge, Gowan, Nagle, Nogle, Rotchford, Sangster, Songster, Thornhull, Thurston.
13. Keane.
14. Batten, Francklyn, Higson, Laborer, Labruer, Mewis, Pycroft.
15. Laforey.

PLATE 11.

1. Wakeham.
2. Cookson, Ivey, Staff, Wagstaff, Viell.
3. Wakeman.
4. Yate.
5. Wake.
6. Aldersey, Alderson, Nonwike.
7. Aldirford, Slauter.
8. Yaldwyn.
9. Alford, Espinasse, Gough, Hill, Newbold, Sandford.
10. Bairstow, Bristow.
11. Alfounder.
12. Baker.
13. Baker.
14. Bainbridge, Bainbrigge.
15. Bard, Beard.

PLATE 12.

1. Ashman, Balfour, Belfore, Belfour, Belfoure, De la River, Delariver, Laverin.
2. Abarough, Abarow, Atbarough, Atborough, Crew, Dalley, Daly, Glen, Glenn, Judd, Jude, Lowe, Watmough, Watmoughe.
3. Baad, Bad, Goldesborough, Goldsbrough, Puller, Turbott, Turbutt.
4. Ginger, Maxwell.
5. Adderbury, Almack, Almanerlaval, Bogle, Caddel, Cantrell, Carden, Carfrae, Cheslin, Clemsby, Crammond, Devereux, Fauze, Fawconer, Haveland, Higginson, Kestell, Lang, Leveale, Levealis, M'Allum, M'Clean, Macknight, M'Knight, Maclean, M'Lean, M'Naughtan, Macnaughton, M'Naughton, M'Naugton, Malcolm, Malcom, Maples, Town of Marlborough; Mason, Masons, Merrick, Meyrick, Orton, Pardeo, Pardoe, Parsons, Pearson, Poor, Reed, Schapmar, Stables, Thorlby, Thorley, Torre, Tournay, Towers, Turney, Whiteman, Whitingham, Wintersells.
6. Calder, Dun, Dunn, Evington, Evinton, Gordon, Klee.
7. Acres, Acris, Dagget, Mawbey, Mawbrey.
8. Botevile, Boteville, Bonteville, Clesby, Dacasta, Da Costa, Maynstone, Mead, Raynsford, Steede, Thynne.
9. Arderne, Anderson, Beauchampe, Berney, Blofeld, Boyd, Boyde, Broughton, Capel, Capell, Carpenter, De Costa, Douglas, Dyne, Dynne, Eden, Edon, Edwards, Egerton, Enys, Giberne, Grentmesnell, Latimer, Lerouox, Mompesson, Mompisson, Montpenston, Phillpot, Relham, Relhan, Rothschild, Shardelou, Stoteville, Tame, Windus.
10. Abelon, Abilon, Barclay, Eadon, Harding, Hardy.
11. Addison, Beamish, Bemish, Cass, Faal, Lawder, Pashley, Pasley.
12. Bower, Falcon, Fawcon, Newfoundland Company.
13. Chaucer, Chauser, Chawcer, De Rivers, De Ryvers, Gaven.
14. Booth, Carnegy, Carnegy-Lindsay, Crooks, Crucks, De Courcy, Dickens, Gairdner, Hume, Jaffray, Mare, Marsh, Passmere, Shields, Spark, Sparke, Syms.
15. Barsham, Denny, Hagar, Lambard, Lambarde, Prelate, Toulmin, Wever, Williams.

PLATE 13.

1. Ferrers, Stewart.
2. Longlands, Newce, Newse.
3. Ferrier.
4. Bradley, Crathorne, Felding, Fielden, Hopkins, Huger, Macfarlane.
5. Inwards, Laurin, Parsons.
6. Fiske, Fyshe.
7. Gascoyne.
8. Dun, Dunne, Gardner.
9. Alwaye, Gaylien.
10. Campbell, Hauger.
11. Gerdon.
12. Hartwell.
13. Hartridge.
14. Gibbon.
15. Heath.

PLATE 14.

1. Davall, Davell, Haldane, Nairne, Oakley, Playfair.
2. Achym, Acklame.
3. Blennerhasset, Carlyon, Corby, Hawks, Paganell, Pagnell, Trewarther.
4. Algar, Alger, Hully, Randolph, Vinicombe.
5. Cash, Gaille, Groombridge, Hitchens, Hitchins, Hyland, Jennings, Quested.
6. Abrook, Abrooke, Adams, Allix, Andrade, Barry, Barton, Beath, Bery, Blackie, Blaikie, Booer, Borminghall, Bower, Budworth, Burghall, Causton, Clerke, Cliffe, Clopton, Coddington, Delahey, Donne, Dounies, Duane, Ellick, Flood, Gildea, Gower, Grene, Guly, Hammond, Hamond, Hampton, Hanna, Heygate, Highgate, How, Ilinn, Isherwood, Jefferson, Jennings, Kendall, Kenerby, Lediard, Liddiat, Lidiard, Lloyd, Lovet, Lovett, Lowe, Lupton, M'Queen, Maingy, Manners, Methuen, Methven, Middleton, Miller, Moody, Moodye, Morton, Norie, Norrie, Norton, O'Duane, Pigot, Pigott, Pratt, Prentice, Prittie, Quin, Rush, Rushe, Seaton, Sharpe, Smallpece, Smalpece, Smallpiece, Stiddolph, Sutton, Trelawney, Troutback, Troutbeck, Waldoure, Ward-Lucas-Touch, Warde, White, Wilbraham, Worseley, Worsley, Wynne.
7. Parkes, Radford, Turnour.
8. Blacker, Drury, Foliot, Foliott, Harwine, Jenkins, Luxmore, Misserinen, Missirinen, Morse, Norton, Radcliffe, Shinglehurst, Waddell, Weddel, Weddell.
9. Day, Derham, Downer, Flinn, Lidel, Raynor.
10. Albany, Beresford, Casaer, De Rouillon, Durham, Fortun, Gillun, Guilam, Gwillam, Hambley, Hambly, Lyssers, Lyzzers, Roclay, St. Andrea, St. Andrew, Sherlock, Smith, Smythe, Vandeput, Whitington, Wynne.
11. Abadain, Abaudain, Auvray, Blaumester, Bowerbank, Brian, Brisbane, Bryan, Douglas, Drake, Emline, Emlyn, Gordon, Grant, Harty, Leahy, Levingstone, Mackenzie, Meally, Meriton, Murray, Powel, Powell, Sabben, St. Owen, Shaw, Spilman, Stewart, Trumpeter, Wightman, Willingham, Wood, Woodd.
12. De Burgh, Dixon, Fayt, Gucheres, Hardgrave, Hardgrove, Harman, Mack, Nettlefold, Plummer, Ross, St. Low, Sproul, Whitbread, Wilson.

PLATE 14—*continued.*

13. Dorn, Gardiner, Matravers, Tackle, Tobin, Undall.
14. Atwood, Bonham, Boymen, Boyham, Boynam, Copson, Lefever, Lefevre, Tait, Whittaker.
15. Buggen, Buggens, Buggin, Conran, Cranston, Hendly, Temple.

PLATE 15.

1. Abarle.
2. Aber, Fletcher, Kayle, Purefey, Thomason.
3. Abbis, Abbiss, Abis, Abys, Asloum, Johnston, Johnstone, Ruddiman, Trail.
4. Babb, Babe, Boyd, Dennie, Denny, Dingham, Logan.
5. Backhouse, Bywater, Carbinell, Ferron, Mays, Rolls.
6. Aberkirdor, Aberkirdour, Bagge, Baillie, Dunn, Fowlis, Gibb, Gorham, Jarrett, Kier, Lyster, Tay, Wilby.
7. Cage, Manley, Manly.
8. Acbiche, Aceck, Arbuthnot, Archdale, Barclay, Cheyne, Feron, Forbes, Fouk, Hackbeck, Mersar, Rossie, Tritton.
9. Bone, Campbell.
10. Adelsorf, Brand, Campbell, Dacoomb, De Spencer, Despencer, Fitz-Raynard, Graham, Maxton, Melvill, Melville, Raynold, St. Denouac, Woodhead.
11. Dacres, Somersett.
12. Dalglish, Garden, Grant, Hamilton, Harmer, Hill, M'Donald, Menzies, Pollock, Sprewell; Stationers' Trade, London; Umphray, Warner, Wheldale, Wmphrey.
13. Birch, Buckner, Burgh, Crooke, Eady, Hartstronge, Jackson, Rowlands.
14. Bathurst, Cochrane, Cochran, Colt, Craddock, Cradock, East, Fuller, Gernon, Giron, Jackson, Jeys, Killach, Lent, Lochead, Lochhead, M'Cullock, Nethercoat, Plumett, Plunket, Plunkett, Steel, Trayton, Treton, Tritton, Trotter, Whitacre, Whitaker.
15. Burton, Cramer, Crammer, Eccles, Eyre, Fitz-Herbert, Gringfield, Grudgfield, Meldert, Millman, Seaton, Slater, Wegge.

PLATE 16.

1. Cocke, Donelan, Eyres, Fabian, Macdougall, Millward, Powis, Powys, Trewarthen, Umfreville.
2. Cock, Ray.
3. Akelits, Akelitz, Fauntleroy, Hakelut, Hemstead, Hemsted, Tilley, Tunnadine.
4. Arthure, Curwen, Gabriel, Gabryell.
5. Bradfield, Corfield, Gairden, Jacomb, Maude, Ockley.
6. Bucketon, Buckton, Buketon, Fassett, Garmston, Molton, Moulton.
7. Hachet, Hacket.
8. Accorne, Adson, Aikenhead, Aikman, Aitkenhead, Akenhead, Anderson, Anketell, Asterby, Braidwood, Brantingham, Brentingham, Cunningham, Dackcombe, Deinston, Dufrene, Elliot, Elliott, Falstoffe, Forrest, Gordon, Gordon-Taylor, Grant, Halliday, Hamilton, Hog, Hogue, Hurst, Kesstell, Kinnimond, Latta, Leeks, Leving, Lilley, M'Crae, Macrea, Mayn, Mendorf, Morton, Muirside, Nigell, Nigill, Pix, Ponton, Righton, Ronald, Roots, Rowntree, Scardlow, Smith, Smollett, Southey, Taylor, Templeton, Thrale, Threele, Tierney, Titterton, Tree, Warley, Wilding, Wood, Woolrych.
9. Amcot, Amcotes, Amcots, Amcotts, Ash, Baldwin, Barzey, Bloundell, Bluett, Blundell, Burles, Cresswell, Dowsing, Feauliteau, Forest, Gilbard, Gilbert, Greyndour, Harvye, Haslewood, Hillersden, Hillesden, Holt, Littler, Loveday, Lovell, Mervyn, Newhouse, Nicholls, Perceval, Skerritt, Smithson, Thynne, Tippets, Vavasour, Wilson, Woodgate, Woodnoth, Woodward, Yeates.
10. Abercrombie, Abercromby, Abernethy, Aiken, Aiscough, Aitken, Aitkine, Allan, Cheyne, Corse, Crosse, Dobbie, Dobie, Ellison, Feyrey, Feytrey, Foulis, Gabriel, Garen, Gordon, Guthrie, Ironside, Leith, Lovayne, Loveyne, M'Cleish, Marr, Mitchell, Moffat, Newall, Petrie, Radnor, Redham, Robe, Spalding, Thrale.
11. Baillie, Baird, Bayly, Burdenbroke, Burnet, Bushey, Bushy, Campbell, Chisalme, Chisholme, Clive, Cruickshanks, Davis, Dennet, Downie, Duncan, Edwards, Ffoulkes, Geike, Gordon, Gourlay, Gourlee, Gourley, Halliday, Hamilton, Hughes, Hunter, Innes, Jones, Lockhart, Loftus, Longford, Lorn, Lurford, M'Donald, M'Tavish, Myers, Nisbet, Nisbett, Oates, Parnell, Phillip, Powell, Purcell, Sanders, Smart, Soulsby, Spence, Swinfen, Taplen, Torrell, Urquhart, Verschoyle, Wallace, Waring, Whittuck, Yonge.
12. Backie, Baikie, Dart, Darte, Dast, Firebrae, Graham, Walles, Wallis.
13. Baillie, Brigid, Farquhar, Ferquhar, Inglis, Johnston, Kerioll, Lightbody, Sinclair, Southcote, Steddert, Stoddart, Taddy.
14. Bracy, Campbell, Nathan.
15. Archbald, Archibald, Crawford, Dolan, Grendon, Haxton, Jeanes, Jeans, Mikieson.

PLATE 17.

1. Ferguson, Glover, Illingsworth, Illingworth.
2. Amphlett, Amphlet, Cardinal, Goldfinch, Howel, Howell, Oliphant.

PLATE 17—*continued.*

3. Farrar, Farrer, Farror, Ferrier, Gradock, Gradocke, Warne.
4. Murle, Minchin, Raparus.
5. Barker, Gleave, Hamilton, Meddop, Neish, Round, Tully.
6. Henley.
7. Greenall, Guinners, Hecter, Hepworth, Hutchings, Ligonier, Thornton.
8. Graham, Moir, Scot.
9. Alden, Bass, Bylteel, D'Ayley, D'Oyley, Eredy, Felton, FitzAmond, Folton, Johnson, Otway, Tanke, Van Straubenzee.
10. Henderson.
11. Heriz.
12. Hearle, Lammie, L'Amy, Lavers, Prior.
13. Allden, Alldin, Alldon, Grantham.
14. Elston, Heselrigge, Hogan, Mayor, Shipey, Shippey, Tracey.
15. Gascoign.

PLATE 18.

1. Abborne, Balfour, Colquhoun, Haggard, Harrow, Lamont, Newberry, Newbery, Ryan, Ussher.
2. Abden, Banester, Dikes, Dykes.
3. Abbot, Abbott, Gregor, Kennedy.
4. Abingdon, M'Kenzie.
5. Donaldson, Greenough, Illsley.
6. Akarys, Akaster, Antram, Aspinall, Aspinwall, Aunger, Aveline, Ballantyne, Ballard, Bannatyne, Blackman, Blackmane, Blackmore, Boyer, Bradfoot, Braidfoot, Bradfute, Browne, Canning, Cater, Chadborn, Chatterton, Chester, Cockshutt, Collins, Cuff, Diddier, Didear, Dodson, Dolby, Dolseby, Dugdale, Dupuy, Eveleigh, Follet, Forsyth, Garde, Gardiner, Garvagh, Gillam, Godfrey, Grantham, Greenhill, Grimshaw, Hall, Hancocke, Holmes, Holroyd, King, Lane, Leathes, Leslie, Lester, Lewis, Lowe, M'George, M'Haffie, Majorebanks, Majoribanks, Marjoribanks, Meverell, Morrall, Morwell, Mounstephen, Mountsteven, Neagle, Newcourt, Newmarch, Orme, Page, Pares, Pateshall, Peers, Pigeon, Randall, Reeves, Regan, Rix, Rosson, Russell, Scot, Scott, Shadwell, Steadman, Swayne, Thompson, Twiss, Waller, Waters.
7. Bonney, Cabell, Fakenham, Feckenham, Fitz-Ralph.
8. Boddington, Bodington, Cahill, Scrimzeor, Scrymzeor, Wedderburn.
9. Balbirney, Baldberney, Bambrough, Bambury, Boult, Callagan, Callagham, Hopcroft, Pagelet.
10. Acorne, Aikman, Aitkenhead, Akenhead, Anderson, Asburner, Aserburne, Asherburne, Ashburner, Ellames, Haliburton, Hensley, Larra, Redfern, Rinton, Tankard.
11. Claxton.
12. Balfour, Blagrove, Blagrave, Cairns, Dyton, Fielding, Fleeming, Gariock, Hamil Hammill, Leghton, Lighton, Newbigging, Place, Pulley, Sandilands, Spashott, Stysted.
13. Ayloffe, Dales, Dalles, Froyle, Guyat Hamill, Ivers, Jevers, Legh, Lukin, Partridge, Peard, Penney, Slaning, Slanning, Treby, Wastneys, Young.
14. Achyem, Adam, Alderton, Anderson, Arnet, Arnot, Arnott, Arnut, Baillie, Balfour, Bestow, Blair, Burnside, Stirling, Dalhurst, Dallas, Dobbie, Ferney, Gilchrist, Gordon, Hamilton, Hodgers, Hollingworth, Holyoke, Kidd, Killgour, Kilgowr, Kinnear, Kydd, Leask, Leslie, Lucie, Mackenzie, MacNicol, Melville, Melvill, Melvill-Whyte, Menzies, Mikison, Motherwell, Myrtoun, Oliphant, Otter, Papillon, Percey, Perwiche, Powe, Rider, Romorley, Romilly, Scot, Scougal, Seaton, Seton, Simpson, Sommerville, Souter, Stiven, Tottenham, Trent, Trinling, Watt.
15. Albon, Albone, Allebone, Allibone, Dana, Gosnall, Gosnold, Kimber, Veitch.

PLATE 19.

1. Alkewe, Askue, Ayskew, Alpin, Ashworth, Ayskey, Bangor, Borthwick, Boston, Brackenbury, Briscoe, Briscowe, Buller, Charlewood, Charlwood, Creswell, Crofton, Duston, Dustone, Greathead, Harlaw, Irby, Johnson, Lang, Laverye, Ligon, Macnab, M'Nab, Maxwell, Medcalf, More, Moubray, Mure-William, Penhelleke, Powtrell, Pykin, Rayley, Rideout, Ridout, Roughead, Saint-Lo, Salwey, Savage, Shelton, Strelley, Webbe-Weston, Williams.
2. Arsick, Arsike, Arsycke, Arsyke, Coock, Cook, Crompton, Laughlin, Metcalf, Metcalfe.
3. Acher, Ager, Auger, Ancher, Anchor, Anke, Ankor, Archer, Awger, Beaumont, Beverley, Bluck, Borman, Bowerman, Bulkeley, Bull, Burnman, Cole, Francoys, Grimes, Haughton, Haville, Hawton, Howgart, Ingram, Ledsam, Lowfield, M'Clean, Meare, Mylie, Noone, Noune, Nun, Nunn, Nunne, Ogle, Oldaker, Saunders, Sheppard, Southern, Southwerth, Southworth, Stark, Stork, Studdert, Torrance, Turnbull, Wharton, Wickham, Williams, Woodrof, Woodrow.
4. Archer.
5. Desbarres, Fowke, M'Gileoun, MacGilleoun.
6. Blackwill, Bonvill, Fisher, Fulcher, Halliday, Miles, Peck, Shields, Trant, Twedie.
7. Tiller.
8. Bosgrave, Burbage, Burbyche, Fenrother.
9. Bold, Bolourd, Bontien, Palliser, Frin,

PLATE 19—*continued.*

Slaughter, Washington, Whatton, Whitcomb.
10. Byers, Grieve, Kymberlee, Kymberley, Moses, Shum, Tame.
11. Broomfield, Butterworth, Incleden, Ingleton.
12. Bie, By, Bye, Fermour, Hamilton, Lingham, Mackie.
13. Clive, Cother, Delsume, Greene, Radborne, Tollemache, Tomb, Werden, Wolridge, Wolrige.
14. Barne, De Grey, Don, Donn, Robinson, Shee.
15. Beaufey, Beaufoy, Cholmley, Hanam.

PLATE 20.

1. Abbat, Basset, Bonnet, Carleton, Carrington, Collyer, Colyear, Conyngham, Coore, Cullowe, Cuninghame, Cunningham, Cunynghame, Daniel, Daniell, Dobbs, Elliot-Fogg, Ensor, Every, Fairlie, Fairly, Filioll, Flower, Fogg, Fogge, Fogo, Folshurst, Foulshurst, Freeling, Fulleshurst, Gale, Gillespie, Gilmer, Gorwood, Gunthorpe, Gurwood, Gyves, Head, Kemeys, Kitson, Knott, Law, Leigh, Man, Mille, Oliphant, Peirce, Pery, Peterkin, Phillott, Pilliner, Piper, Poulett, Pownall, Ramsay, Ramsey, Richardson, Ritchie, Sherborne, Sherburne, Shirborne, Sladden, Stewart, Trevithick, Wilkinson, Wombwell.
2. Abcot, Abcott, Foxton, Fraser, Gleig, Hoole, Lehoop, Mortimer, Mortymer, Plantagenet, Plantaginet.
3. Aboril, Abrol, Plaiz, Playse, Wakeman, Wettyn, Wettyng.
4. Babeham, Babehaw.
5. Bacon, Forster, Gregory, Ridpath, Wall, Whyt.
6. Aickinson, Aitkenson, Bailey, Baylee, Bailie, Bailey. Elphinstone.
7. Abbey, Campbell, Abday, Abdey, Abdy, Ainslie, Alison, Allison, Anderson, Albins, Argentre, Argentree, Aubrey, Awbrey, Baird, Baynton, Bishop, Borke, Brown, Browne, Brunneck, Bund, Busfield, Campbell, Darby, Datmer, Ellison, Feld, Fontain, Fontaine, Forbes, Furlong, Gardner, Gilfillian, Gleneagees, Glyn, Goodsir, Graham, Guybyon, Hacket, Hadden, Haldane, Halden, Hamden, Hampden, Hennidge, Hide, Jackson, Jollyffe, Keay, Kindon, Kingdon, Lewis, Lidderdale, M'Fall, M'Fell, MacKennal, MacKannal, M'Kindlay, Mackinlay, Maclure, M'Lure, Madam, Merydale, Mittlewell, Monro, Morgan, Newbery, Phillips, Pickard, Princep, Ramsbotton, Screggs, Scroggs, Scrymgeour, Shuckforth, Simpson, Simson, Sleigh, Smedly, Somner, St. Clair-Erskine, St. Quintin, Theed, Timmins, Tonkin, Torin, Wedderbourn, Wedderburn, Wyberg.
8. Cannyngs, Carnagie, M'Mahon.
9. Bussell, Cranston, Cranstoun, Fennison, Fythey, Fythie, Hale, Kinder, Kutchin, O'Hara, Ryley, Waring.
10. Dabbins.
11. Dale.
12. Aphe, Amy, Dalston.
13. Birmingham, Dobson, Dodson, Littledale, M'Donall, M'Dowgal.
14. Amyas, Amys, Bisshe, Crotty, Davoron, Grogan, Hatton Jephson, Lecky, Leigh, M'Donald, Parr, Prickett, Seymour, Welstead, Welsted, Welstod, Yardeley.
15. Calthorp, Delaval, Douglas, Dundas, Ebhert, Fitz-Harbert, Gill, Goddard, Shaftow, Smight, Smyth, Smiggs, Townsend.

PLATE 21.

1. Abbot, Barret, Brereton, Cloude, Yaxley.
2. Abenhall, Ablehall, Phipps.
3. Acham, Acklame, Boardman, Brough, Grys, Lennox, Pendarves, Philips, Phillips.
4. Abel, Abell, Brigg, Gamin, Wilton.
5. Bagne, Bagul, Cromwell, Lomas, Playfair, Spooner, Vincent.
6. Alston, Andrew, Baillie, Bruce, Carnagie, Carnegie, Dayrolles, Graham, Haggard, Jeffrey, Langdell, Pink, Pinck, Sackville, Scot, Scott, Seton, Walkington.
7. Burton, Booth, Campbell, Gordon, Ingilby, Jones, Kirk, Kirke, Kitto, Kittoe, Lashmar, Loftus, Lundie, M'Queen, Middleton, Newton, Raison, Ralegh, Rayment, Reason, Robson, Swinhoe, Terry, Tichbourne, Tollemache, Weale, Whichcote, Whichcot, Wrottesley.
8. Carnaghi, Carnagie, Carnegie, Carnegy, Holgrave, Holgreve, Hulgrave, Moderby, Sievewright, Sievwright.
9. Alford, Barrow, Cassie, Calclough, Colcloughe, Colvil, Colville, Dicconson, Dickens, Fydell, Handby, Harpden, Heriet, Jennet, Jennett, Katerley, Montgomery, Moynley, Noton, Pattison, Pyrry, Railton, Richardson, Stockley, Tallant, Thwaites, Underwood, Whitebread, Whiteway, Wingate, Woodriff, Yardley.
10. Alexander, Arcedeckne, Bragge, Broge, Brogg, Broige, Bruce, Buchanan, Bunten, Clevland, Coddington, Cumine, Cumming, Dalmahoy, Dogherty, Doherty, Donaldson, Dotson, Dunlop, Durno, Duthie, Erskine, Fry, Gardiner, Gay, Gerdelley, Gerdilly, Gillanders, Gleig, Gordon, Groseth, Guthrie, Gunn, Davine, Dickson, Hart, Kennedy, Linning, Livingston, Livingstone, Lizurs, M'Aul, M'Breid, M'Call, M'Crae, M'Cray, Mackenzie, M'Kenzie, M'Nab, Meres, More, Muire, Mure, Neasmith, Neill, Neylan, Nixon,

PLATE 21—*continued.*

O'Dogherty, O'Duire, O'Dwire, Ogilvie, O'Gorman, O'Hart, O'Neylan, Oxtoby, Parker, Peart, Perring, Peterson, Pillans, Rains, Rashleigh, Readers, Riky, Romanes, Salmon, Scholey, Seaton, Sharples, Sibbald, Spiers, Stewart, Stuart, Thom, Walmsley, Whetwell, Whitacre.

11. Abernethy, Dick, Donkin, Drummond, Duncan, Hamilton, Harkness, Leckie.
12. Denistoun, Dennestoun.
13. Cassan, Chamond, Chaumond, Crag, Cragg, Edmonds.
14. Elves, Elwes, Hale, Hales, Halles, Vandeleur, Woodburgh.
15. Breawse, Burden, Ewart, Forbes, Forster.

PLATE 22.

1. Adney, De Pudsey, Eaton, Greenlaw, Lighton, Linton, Skelton.
2. Adam, Adams, Addams, Adeane, Dingdale, Dugdale, Short, Shorter, Willans.
3. Cooper, Jeffreys.
4. Baring, Jury, Lovejoy, M'Kall.
5. Addey, Addy, Barkeley, Buckland, Freshfield, Furser, Furzer, Kinsman, Mansel, Nix.
6. Parker.
7. Aneys, Carbonel, Carbonell, Forbes, Ogilvie, Ogilvy, Sterry.
8. Arden, Arderne, Ardyn, Barron, Canton, Crenway, Devere, Fillingham, Fitzgerald, Harding, Humffreys, Vere, Wynne.
9. Bourdon, Burdon, Cardiff, Chadwick, Jermain, Jermayne, Livingston, Livingstone, Moncrief, Reding, Stewart, Watson.
10. Crackanthorpe, Doyne.
11. Aglionby, Agneu, Agnew, Aidgman, Allanson, Allanson-Winn, Baron, Birch, Booker, Carnegie, Cheltenham, Cockman, Deacons, De Ufford, Dixon, Dopping, Elson, Flounders, Greaves, Grellier, Hampton, Keble, Mitton, Moxon, Newbury, Oldfield, Otway, Perkins, Petrie, Ramsay, Snelling, Stephens, Tarrant, Wadman, Waithman, Wymond.
12. Angoleme, Boggis, Boggs, De Angolesm, Exton, Marston, Maston, Tennant.
13. Dicey, Duval, Duvall, Edwin, Foley, Jesse, Pellott, Pillett, Pillott.
14. Cumine, Cumming, Ellacot, Ellicott, Enderbie, Enderby, Gawden, Glanvile, Glanville, Lord, Lorimer, Robarts.
15. Ashendeu, Ashondon, Brackley, Egerton, Haxford, Moul, Moule.

PLATE 23.

1. Adair, Edington, Macalpin, Molleson, Munt, Musard, Roddam, Tiddeman, Tideman.
2. Aiton, Aitoune, Angeville, Angevine, Anvers, Baker, Cashen, Chambre, Clason, Classon, Delap, English, Hailstones, Kingsford, Limesie, Meignell, Rochfort, Rodatz, Rome, Ross, Stevenson, Tilly, Wheeler, Wiley.
3. Ash, Aske, Bayn, Conyers, Norton, Selby, Topper.
4. Bake, Bannerman, Bonekill, Borrowman, Bunsfield, Chassereau, Crossdaile, Durborough, Easton, Elliot, Elliott, Giles, Geils, Le Hunt, Ogilvie, Sale, Trew.
5. Andby, Andy, Andey, Banck, Banke, Banks, Colthurst, Faith, Jeffreys, Standon.
6. Bisset, Boughs, Bush, Bushe, Bussche, Falkner, Holbeach, Twining.
7. Burnet, Calderwood, Caldron, Caldwood, Calwood, Caunter, Ecton, Elder, Fidler, Krampton, Kranton, Maynard, Montgomery, Ogilvie, Ogilvy, Palmes, Seagrave, Seagrove, Shiers, Willmott.
8. Amyand, Baillie, Bazilie, Bazely, Corbet, Corbett, Craw, Cromer, Johns, La Roche, Magrath, Orchard, Talbot-Rice, Thurlow.
9. Dodsworth, Montgomery, Purefoy, Smyth, Tidcombe, Watkins.
10. Dalziel, Dobbs, Dod, Dode, Somervile, Somerville.
11. Yarde.
12. Almears, Almeers, Ameers, Comries, M'Glashan, Massingham.
13. Byirley, Fyvie, Heather, Holles, Peirson, Pym, Urquhart, Vaughan.
14. Crog, Crogg, Ede, Marnham, Vario.
15. Adlard, Arnot, Arrat, Arrot, Barclay, Bayn, Binney, Binny, Carr, Chisholme, Clarke, Coape, Cocke, Coke, Collow, Crabtree, Donaldson, Douglas, Durno, Eccleston, Eclestone, Erskine, Ferguson, Fitchet, Forbes, Gelstable, Gillet, Goodenough, Graham, Grant, Gray, Gosset, Gossett, Hamilton, Hardie, Hotoft, Hotofte, Houston, Keir, King, Kyrklot, Lamond, Leeky, Lurty, Lyell, M'Caa, M'Caskill, M'Donald, M'Dowal, M'Entire, Macgregor, M'Intyre, Mackay, M'Quie, Menteath, Naish, Pagan, Paterson, Pearce, Peitere, Peter, Picard, Pillans, Primrose, Reay, Reoch, Rymer, Stewart, Stobart, Toll, Tolle, Tonyn.

PLATE 24.

1. Aberbuthnet, Arburthnot, Brounlee, Brownlee, Bronlie, Burman, Fitz-Barnard, Gemell, Gemill, Gemmell.
2. Abercorne, Burn, Garside, Gartside, Hair, Littell, Noy, Thirwell, Wakerley.
3. Aberdeen, Cantwell, Cunningham, Hay,

PLATE 24—*continued.*

Hereford, Huggins, Love, Nottingham, Scot, Scott, Wager, Wastley.
4. Badcock, Cavanagh, Dickson, Eveleigh, Maxwell, Sodon.
5. Bagnel, Bagnell, Bagnill, Bagnoll, Esclabor, Gospatrick, Hailly, M'Gowan, M'Nabb.
6. Baillie, Brutton, Bruzead, Burke, Dick, Jelter, M'Bean, M'Gilevray, Mackintosh, Mackpherson, Macpherson, M'Pherson, Milles, Palmer, Rickard, Sutherland.
7. Amenton, Atwood, Blackburn, Calamount, Chyner, Lingwood.
8. Callandar, Callender, Cleves, Culliford, Fittz, Roscoe, Steinmetz.
9. Ballenden, Cairns, Craufurd, Crawford, Gwyn, Newbigging, Wickliff, Wyckliffe.
10. Alphe, Dalston, Fearon, Mandley, Martyn.
11. Bloss, Dalley, Daly, Dally, Kathyng, Kating, Katting, Kaytyng, Leslie.
12. Carter, Crenage, Crenidge, Dan, Dann, Gove, Sheldon.
13. Deycourt, Dunnage, Eardley, Griggs, Panton, Sheircliff, Shiercliffe, Tournemine.
14. Bodwida, Bowida, Busfield, Cassils, Crook, Eastland, Estland, Estlin, Fowne, Newborough, Plafair, Vaughan.
15. Erisby.

PLATE 25.

1. Aberdour, Ariel, Ariell, Coningham, Fitz-Ourse, Furnival, Furnivall, Paveley, Topham.
2. Abernethy, Boreston, Borreston, Danyers, Fairfowl, Farbridge, Goodchild, Lethieullier, Lethulier, Parrot, Parrott, Pearson, Peerson, Perrot, Pierson, Senhouse, Tarbock.
3. Aberkirdor, Cannon, Goold, Gould, Jewers, Leslie, Tregos.
4. Bageley, Bagley, Dawes, Daws.
5. Badham, Baillie, Brignall, Jerard, Jerrard, Tovey, Zorks.
6. Bevile, Bookey, Bradbury, Comberford, Dowie, Durie, Dury, Foulis, Gordon, Heron, Hull, Narbon, Othwell, Sheddan, Wrangham.
7. Carruthers, Croudace, Duffy, Murray, Preston, Standen.
8. Calender, Callander.
9. Beringer, Christie, Handcock, Hendey, Hendy.
10. Benson, Bosum, Davy, Devereulx, Goode, Laver.
11. Baines, Bone, Dempster, Gall, Hodkinson.
12. Couldwell, Downe, Farmingham, Lawrence, Luxmoore, Luxmore, Mauger, Molloy, Newenton, Simmons, St. Lawrence.
13. Arneel, Arneil, Arnied, Boors, Delamare, Dunkin, Ellis, Foy, Phillips, Shipton.
14. Deveral, Deverel, Emerson, Tytler.
15. Allaway, Alloway, Ancram, Bridges, Brunton, De la Cherois, Gray, Grieve, Hiching, Kinnear, Longland, Longlands, Ormistone, Petrie, Pitcairn, Rait, Roberton, Smith, Spence, Stainforth, Stedman, Steedman, Yoe.

PLATE 26.

1. Ainsley, Ainslie, Beggar, Fisher, Godfrey, Grieves, Henrie, Jeffs, Ketchin, Kitchin, Machen, Peaterson, Sprott, Stratoun, Tillotson.
2. Achieson, Aitchison, Anwell, Anwyl, Anwyll, Atcheson, Jordan, Lancelot, Lockyer, Peche, Pechey.
3. Archer, Crawford, Kennedy, Niven.
4. Balderstone, Balderston, Balderstoun, Bauderstone, Bauderston, Bennet, Cornelius, Donald, Geney, Genny, Jeny, Myreton, Myrtoun.
5. Balfour.
6. Bentham, Valence, Valomess.
7. Audin, Ayde, Chedworth, Fortune, Harly, Hene, Henne, Rickets, Ricketts, Wall.
8. Alexander, Chambers, Cleghorn, Norse, Pope, Renny, Tuirmins.
9. Blamire, Blaumire, Boorne, Burgon, Carrell, Ceely, Ciely, Colbrand, Forde, Gilman, Greenwood, Nevill, Thetford, Townrawe, Waldron, Waldrond.
10. Acton, Andson, Ashlin, Bertie, Bradburne, Bradbourne, Christall, Coffin-Pine, Cogan, Commolin, Hunter, M'Gregor, Noy, Pyne, Walsam, Walsham, Willington.
11. Broese, Brookman, Denham, Gattie, Gatty, Pettyt, Petyt, Sotheram.
12. Atkinson, Atchinson, Belward, Bykenor, Carden, Chabnor, Clark, Clarke, Clerke, Davidson, De Ferrers, Dragoner, Drayner, Drummond, Ferrers, Hansby, Helme, Holt, Huthwait, Kirkwood, Lewellyn, Llewellyn, Mudge, Mudie, Nichols, Plater, Raeburn, Sall, Sharp, Smart, Spinks, Sydney.
13. Alexander, Anderson, Baillie, Don, Elphingston, Gamage, Hamilton, Huddlestone, Keith, Lealy, Mitchell, Paterson, Patterson, Popkin, Scott, Screvener, Scrivener, Scrivenor, Smith, Sym, Whyttuck, Whytock, Young.
14. Baynard, Buchanan, Clubb, Collyer, Criktoft, Cunningham, Elder, Every, Horniold, Hornyold, Mauington, Northey, Sampaye.
15. Drake.

PLATE 27.

1. Aberton, Aburton, Cuthbert, Cuthburt, Gratton, Latouche, Moore.
2. Aberdwell, Abredrobell, Henden, Inglebert, Kennedy, Mawson, Molloy, Pateis.
3. Abeline, Ablin, Ablyn, Dransfield, Ireby, Knapman, Maclellan, Murdoch, Sheen.
4. Bain, Barcas, Barkas, Bayne, Corbreake, Corbreyke, Crockford, Hadderwick, Lew, Murray, Murry, Peckam, Peckham, Plenderleith, Purdie, Scot, Stevenson.
5. Baird, Blair, Burns, Collins, Hagen, Hay, Hayes, Lempriere, More, Vallack, Zinzan.
6. Bainbridge, Colladon, Cox, Gaskell, Gaskill, Watson.
7. Calandrine.
8. Bownas, Caldwell, Leale, Leall, Lealle, Segar, Tindal.
9. Apleyard, Appleyard, Barton, Bayford, Boucher, Bouchier, Bredel, Byford, Calverly-Blackett, Calvert, Dover, Gaston, Greseley, Harwood, Horn, Keith, Kirkland, Leeds, Massey, Midford, Savell, Savil, Savile, Savill, Saville, Thorn, Thorne, Woodley, Wynall.
10. Beltead, Belsted, Belstede, Belstide, Dalton, Nottage, Pearse, Rewtoure, Thatcher.
11. Chevalier, Dalsiel, Dalyell, Dalziel, Grill, Hampstead, Hampsted, Hincks, Joice, Joyce, Mount, Widvile.
12. Allaunson, Alyson, Boneham, Bonham, Broadbent, Brodbent, Chamberlain, Chamberlan, Dancer, Leger.
13. Corbet, Dant, Eaten, Eaton, Eton, Rice, Skillicome.
14. Chein, Cheine, Cheyne, De Gaunt, Dorward, Durward, Earnshaw, Mansfield, Matchet, Matcheton, Mercer, Nausolyn, Nottage, Turney.
15. Agneu, Agnew, Egan, Kebell, Keby[ll], Mackillop, M'Killop, Stubbs.

PLATE 28.

1. Abrahams, Balm, Balme, Bollingbroke, Bollingbrook, Bollinsbrook, Slee.
2. Abingdon, Abington, Bult, Cevilioc, Covill, Coville, Girflet, Randell, Randle, Roundel.
3. Abingdon, Achilles, Achillis, Bertie, Bertue, Churchill, Freshacre, Geering, Molcaster, Moncaster, Presland, Prestland, Willoughby.
4. Baines, Bayne, Berrey, Charteris, Clark, Dowine, Dunlop, Finlay, Flanagan, Ganstin, Garstin, Jolleff, Jolliff, Karr, Loftus, Macdonald, Mackenzie, M'Kenzie, Martin, Monteath, Monteith, Neilson, Noble, Rolland, Rowan, Scarth, Skeen, Smith, Stewart, Washborne, Whitelock, Williamson.
5. Gennett.
6. Apifer, Baker, Colliver, Erskine, Inckpen, Inkpen, Proude, Raeburn, Reaburn, Samson, Thornes.
7. Calcraft.
8. Ambros, Ambrose, Ambross, Callandar, Callender, Christie, Coldicott, M'Braid, Patishull, Pattishull.
9. Adventurers, London Hambro' Merchants, Brock, Brownsword, Calmady, Corsar, Corser, Drummond, Finch-Hatton, Michell, Morrison, Nevenham, Nevoy, Newenham, Simon, Swift.
10. Atlee, Atley, Damant, Dwyre, Gameil, Gammill, Hunter, Keunell, Riccaad.
11. Angus, Beatie, Beatty, Cassels, Codd, Codde, Danes, Daneys, Domere, Fox, Freby, Furse, Higgins, Johnson, Lindsay, M'Clen, M'Donald, Malcom, Marris, Meason-Laing, Perry, Portal, Pound, Rawson, Scherlis, Staines, Trevet, Trevett, Turbervill, Turberville.
12. Bulcock, Damerley, Hetherington, Hetherton, Ravis, Roche, Tyrrell.
13. Fowler, Hutton.
14. Clerke, Eaton, Gordon, Hough, Longworth Sandiford.
15. Allvey, Alvey, Farey, Ferrey, Ferry, Hay, Hines, Imbrie, Imrie, Imrey, Kroge, Laugher, Provan, Tane.

PLATE 29.

1. Abriscourt, Abuscourt, Abustourt, Hastday, Joel.
2. Achard, Cracklow, Gates, Seaton, Seton, Willison, Wilson.
3. Ackroyd, Ackeroyd, Akeroyd, Akroyd, Arkroyd, Athell, Crockat, Crockett, Robertson.
4. Baker, Garnett, Gigon, Jorcey, Jorge, Morgan, Pelton, Polton.
5. Bain, Baine, Bidon, Castleman, Pierpont, Pierrepoint, Pierepont.
6. Balderston, Balderstones, Crawford, Crawforde, Downman, Kincaid, Stirling.
7. Agan, Austyn, Brayleaford, Braylford, Dance, Greene, Joule, Stark.
8. Adderton, Aderton, Ainslie, Allardice, Balmanno, Blackwood, Boswell, Brice, Browell, Bruce, Campbell, Carsain, Cobb, Cobbe, Cowper, Dalzell, Dalziel, Dalziell, Damerley, Dammant, Demeschines, Dowglas, Ewart, Foreman, Forman, Gordon, Hamilton, Heart, Heeley, Heely, Inglis, Jollie, Kragg, Lambford, Lamford, Lancaster, M'Aully, M'Haddo, M'Hado, M'Kay, M'Rach, Macrae, Martin, Masterton, Mastertown, Matheson, Meschines, Mowbray, Napier, Nelson, Niblie, Nock, Pim, Rennie, Renny, Sawers, Shortreed, Stewart, Stuart, Weeks, Wemyss.
9. Austrey, Dandern, King, Mellish, Steel, Steele, Trotman, Vallance.
10. Bradeley, Bradley, Edgcumbe, Edgecomb, Haslam.

PLATE 29—*continued.*

11. Bottonley, Edridge, Grandford, Levesque, Trinder.
12. Dobbin, Dodsworth, Edmond, Hagger, Hoy, Hoye, Jumper, Maledoctus, Manduit.
13. Addlington, Adlington, Baker, Bawtre, Bennet, Berkhead, Birmingham, Bowerman, Bowreman, Brooke, Brownlow, Buckton, Bush, Catty, Chetwynd, Clobery, Clowberry, Cokeningham, Cox, Cresswell, Cruttendon, Cuyet, Darrell, Dayrell, Dorrell, Fleeming, Fleming, Frank, Frewke, Garnham, Hands, Hay, Lamplow, Lamplowe, Lamplugh, Leveson, Lewson, Littleboy, Litton, M'Call, Mar, Marm, Marwood, Meredyth, Methoulde, Methwold, Outram, Pritchard, Robley, Ruthven, Sapcotes, Sapcott, Sargent, Shales, Stratford, Sweeting, Temmes, Warde, Wethered.
14. Ainge, Beckley, Beckly, Beykle, Bickley, Bistley, Bystley, Camden, Clarke, Delafield, Dugnall, Henshall, Stert, Whitlock.
15. Camp.

PLATE 30.

1. Symonds, Sadler.
2. Twining.
3. Tylden.
4. Wyrrall.
5. Twemlow.
6. Wright.
7. Weykes, Wykes.
8. Getham, Williams, Wythernewyke.
9. Writington.
10. Swire.
11. Symcoats.
12. Stubbe.
13. Rooper, Roper.
14. Sweet.
15. Ridge.

PLATE 31.

1. Saddler.
2. Barrington, Fursland, Sage, Warner.
3. Crathorne, Sangster.
4. Tasell.
5. Sacker, Saker.
6. Thomas.
7. Tarleton.
8. Scot, Scott.
9. Tatler.
10. Tatum.
11. Scott.
12. Tay.
13. Tharrold.
14. Scrivington.
15. Fort, Forte, MacDonald, Torr.

PLATE 32.

1. Bing, Jowett, Jowitt.
2. Big, Bigg, Bigge, Gilham, Gillham, Mason, Murison, Pearson, Pierson.
3. Ashley, Colemere, Colmore, Humfrey, Hurr, Pocher, Souter, Sutton.
4. Blacke, Brandeston, Bree, Colliver, Hog, Hogg, Kerdiston, Witt.
5. Bill, Bowden, Codd, Fithie, Hagen, Moncrief, Slough, Staller.
6. Blenman, Cummings, Evans, Evers, Kellet, Ring.
7. Cheseldon, Cheseldyne, Coneley, Conelly, Connelley, Connelly, Connely, Connolly, Conolly, Jago.
8. Cheeke, Denison, Wollstonecraft.
9. Abrahall, Cheeke, Calamy, Claxton, Fitz-Harris, Grills, Harris, Hersay, Kempt, Lufers, Mainstone, Maxwell, Mayneston, Speake, Speke, Weedon, Whitwange, Whitwong.
10. Clark, Ince, Kingston.
11. Aher, Aldworth, Clunie, Hauston, Houston, Joass, Syward, Watkinson.
12. Cliffe, Clyff, Clyffe, Gomm.
13. Amidas, Barton, Burnside, Butcher, Coyney, Coyny, Drywood, Hamilton, Jewel, Lindsay, Morrison, St. Maure, Seymour, Sharp, Tibbs, Wood.
14. Althoun, Birn, Brin, Clifford, Cromie, Dunbar, Duncanson, Farquhar, Gayner, Gaynor, Gun, Handasyd, Handyside, Handysyde, Lamond, Lamont, Landen, Lilly, MacFarquhar, Macmorran, Mare, Middleton, Nefmeneill, Nefmenell, Nevenrenell, Patrick, Prescot, Prescott, Sibbald, Watson.
15. Brenan, Brennan, Crane, Howison, Du Boys, Forners, Forneys, Hailes, Hasted, Henderson.

PLATE 33.

1. Ackers, Akers, Alderson, Argahast, Bistley, Bodkin, Cossens, Craig, Craigdallie, Craigie, Crichton, Hurley, Juckes, Jukes, Juxon, Lort, Marrow.
2. Acton, Malefont, Malesaunts.
3. Adamson, Cassidy, Conygors, Darcy, D'Arcy, De Arcy, Evans-D'Arcy, Fitz-Allan, Tidbury.
4. Balfour, Bellett, Bellet, Billet, Billot, Church, Nelson, Nesbett, Nesbitt, Nisbet, O'Hickie, Tipping.
5. Ballett, Brenan, Essex, Estcourt, Halstead,

PLATE 33—*continued.*

Lethbridge, Medlicott, Medlycott, Newcomb, Pagan, Pagenham, Raymond, Strong, Webb.
6. Balnaves, Balneaves, Erdington, Hall, Seth.
7. Calder, Cambell, Campbell, Chamberlain, Chamberlayne.
8. Campbell, Card, Colwick, Colwyke, Kilvington, Lee.
9. Bolt, Boult, Brooke, Bunch, Campbell, Dale, Denton, Farnaby, Gardiner, Graham, Greenhalgh, Greenhaugh, Mathew, Matthews, Moriskines, Pitt, Roebuck, Rote; St. John the Baptist College, Oxford; Starkie, Starkey, Steel, Still, Storer, Storey, Thurston, Torlesse, Upjon.
10. Baylie, Dawbeney, Dawbney, Sinclair, Teulon.
11. Danvers, Davers, Hare, Hester, Hutchinson, Kingswell, Pierce, Ramsay, Soden.
12. Aime, Aine, Binckes, Bincks, Binks, Darlington, Dean, Usher.
13. Edwardes, Edwards, Rawdon, Rich, Wix.
14. Blair, Cobham, Dingley, Dinley, Eddows, Edwardes, Lannoy, Lanoy, Masquenay, Rogers, Symmes, Vance, Whitney.
15. Burbidge, Elam, Hucks, Mackenzie.

PLATE 34.

1. Abeck, Crowe, De Courcy, Elton, Habeck, Kawston, Lupton.
2. Abelyn, Abelyne. Drummond.
3. Abeny, Corry, Erving, Fanning, Fitz-Allen, Heslop, Kingsmill, Leggat, Leggatt, Lutefoote, Vickers.
4. Badger, Bradhull, Brocket, Brockhill, Brockholes, Brockholes - Fitzherbert, Brocklehurst, Broke, Brokelsbey, Brook, Brooke, Brooks, Broughton, Grey, Lambeth, Warner.
5. Campbell, Draper, Foxwell, Gowan, Macrorie, M'Gowan, Ogilvie, Reece, Rolland, Rorie, Ross, Trotter.
6. Baines, Barnes, Garden, Sherlock, Wise.
7. Alexander, Aylet, Bontein, Burrard, Cahan, Cahane, Clayton, Dale, Dollar, Egerton, Forbes, Gallaway, Galloway, Gibthorp, Gibthorpe, Gorman, Griffith, Innes, Jackson, James, Johnson, Keith, Leivy, Lumsden, Luxford, Mackenzie, Macnamara, M'Neil, M'Nelly, O'Cahane, Queade, Skipton, Stewart, Thomond, Waddy, Whyte.
8. Baylis, Burrs, Cain, Caine, Fesant, Gaff, Gateford, Hartley, Hawthorn, Hawthorne, Heard, Kierman, Martin, Porter, Quick, Roope, Voller.
9. Bristed, Campbell, Chuter, M'Kechnie. Powerton.
10. Dalmer, Deleval, Kateler, Kateller, Katheller, Royle.
11. Alison, Allison, Blacket, Blackett, Blaki[illegible], Collison, Collisone, Cotton, Crafford, Craford, Cruickshank, Daisie, Deasie, Elmsey, Fawkne, Halkerston, Halket, Halkett-Craigie-Inglis, Hawker, Hid[illegible], Keyt, Markham, Murphy, Nickolso[illegible], Pirrie, Roos, Ros, Ross, Rudall, Ruddall, Seton, Smither, Stephenson, Twy[illegible], Wright.
12. Ashby, Baggeley, Belgrave, Bilsd[illegible], Chester, Clerke, Copinger, Dalavail, Dalton, Dreux, Gray, Greive, Gre[illegible], Knolas, Knolls, Knowles, Mitton, My[illegible]ton, Pert, Ruthven, Wardman.
13. Aubin, Chitwood, Easens, Ratcliffe, St. Aubin.
14. Cann, Earles, Pie, Pye, Rudde.
15. Beatty, Eastwood.

PLATE 35.

1. Aderson, Foulis, Fowles.
2. A'Court, Bulbec, Bulbeck, De Mohun, Lowe, Sherman, Tapper.
3. Acle, Anhelet, Blackhall, Felfair, Frescheville, Gorges, Gorgis, Lascells, Rivel, Searles.
4. Ball, De Beaumont, Colthurst, Dalgety, Dalgetty, Damory, Ewing, Gates, Halloway, Harnet, Hollowday, Ireland, M'Leish, Mould, Pepper, Royse, Scot, Scott, Thomson.
5. Fraser, Oliphant, O'Selbac, Scollay, Simpson.
6. Bamfield.
7. Campbell, Dudgeon, Grandon, Grandson, Hume, Kearns, Lomax, Macgregor, Orr, Paley, Peters, Watling.
8. Agnew, De Breos, Bruse, Candler, Dethicke, Ramsay, Waters, Weston.
9. Cancelor, Candisheler, Compigne, English, Felter, Laird, Lance, Leny, Paddon, Pugges, Ramsey, Shaw.
10. Curtoys, Dawbin, May, Robertson, Trist,
11. Aiken, Albeney, Atkin, Culchech, Culehech, Dealbeney, Ennis Finderne, Fynderne, Godin, Hay, Hervy.
12. Aikenhead, Aitkenhead, Dansey.
13. Anderson, Bastard, Clarke, Davy, Eliot, Elliot, Elliott, Ellyot, Ellyott, Gardner, Keble, Oliphant, Parker, Putland, Smith, Uvery, Westby, Yate, Yeverey.
14. Cosyn, Duck, Elley, Lydown, Nevell, Whitfield.
15. Areskine, Erskine, Folvill, Folleville, Mann, Parkinson, Toke, Tooke, Tuke.

PLATE 36.

1. Adean, Anne, Avenar, Avenayne, Avenel, Aveneyle, Avenyle, Beech, Bispleam, Blair, Bucknall, Buxton, Calder, Christopher, Clare, Crozier, Domville, D'Oyley, Friend, Gordon, Graham, Griffith, Hay, Heaton, Hulton, Hunter, Hutton, Lacy, Mackenzie, M'Kenzie, Matrevers, Maxwell, Mollesone, Mortimer, Nisbet, Norton, Osmer, Park, Partis, Peckwell, Poole, Pount, Raynsford, Skyrme, Staveley, Steventon, Studley, Sulyard, Taylor, Domville, Thompson, Trye, Wheatley, Windle, Winyard, Worhead.
2. Annat, Annot, Annott, Colton, Durrant, Kelley, Kelly, Keylley, Pollack, Pollarck, Pollock.
3. Abilem, Agas, Agg, Annesley, Audley, Auge, Bruse, Chandos, Chesney, Cleland, Coker, Colamore, Colemere Collmore, Collymore, Conway, Conwy, Cresswell, Creswell, Curling, Everard, Flamank, Flamock, Holles, Howndhile, Lambsey, Lamesey, Ligon, Littleton, Lum, M'Clellan, Masterman, Mordaunt, More, Mores-Rowe, Selby, Shirley, Stirling.
4. Algood, Allgood, Belvale, Gibbons.
5. Adlyn, Bell, Bennet, Dewsbury, Jewssbury, M'Cormack, M'Cormick, Rocke.
6. Bennet, Bennett, Doeg, Giffard, Goldie, Grove, Manson, Pearle, Steuart, Stewart.
7. Colnet, Farlow, Guilford, Haslam.
8. Brownlow-Cecil, Chein, Cheine, Chiene, Loader.
9. Chilworth, Goodhall, Kell, Kelle, Morrall, Vernon.
10. During, Faireborne.
11. Andelby, Dyce, Fortescue, Mervin, Shields, Stopham, Tong, Tonge.
12. Cumine, Cumming, Dusautoy, Gallagher, Geekie, Hayton, Hore, Pyrke, Quatermayne,
13. Archard, Busk, Buske, Fodon, Gascoigne, Hoby, Merritt.
14. Bracy, Bracey, Fair, Hodge, Jelley, Jelly, Wicksted.
15. Archdale, Archedale, Bolden, Dacre, Johnson, Lee, Lennard, Leonard, Malet, Mallet, May, Moyne, Osborne, Stafford, Stubbey, Teys, Tye, Warren.

PLATE 37.

1. Archdeacon, Colliray, Hodington.
2. Anderson.
3. Archer, Athelstane, Keux, Lovise, Neal, Neele.
4. Arnold, Besiles, Besills, Hazlewood, Mein, Silver, Winchester.
5. Boatfield.
6. Aylworth, Freemantle, Mash, Shaw.
7. Berondon, Berondowne, Collier, Collyear, Colyear, Glass, Knowlys, Lecawell, Lodbrook, Lodbrooke, Mutton.
8. Bell, Clinton, De Clinton, Dengaine, D'Engaine, Millard.
9. Beath, Beith, Chrighton, Crichton, Crighton, Howdon, Langrish, M'Gavin, Sugden, Williams.
10. Ayleward, Aylward, Aylwarde, Berry, Brien, Dax, Dore, Foulis, Fowles, Hewet, Holderness, Methven.
11. Bentick, Cromer, Hooton, Kerr, Trotter, Veale.
12. Betagh, Boxhall, Boxmell, Chalbots, Figes, Jourdan, Kadrad, Kinnear, Kinneir, Neefield, Nerfield, Whaley, Wickstead, Wicksted.
13. Armestrang, Armstrang, Armstrong, Bigwood, Fellowes, Fields, Fitz-Symond, Fitz-Water, Hyrson, Lillie, Maddock, Neill, Wodehouse.
14. Bifield.
15. Armour, Arweil, Binns, Clapham, Clepan, Clephan, Eustace, Power, Turing.

PLATE 38.

1. Amias, Amras, Amyas, Bellingham, Blythe, Goulborne, Green, Hicks-Beach, Horsefall, Horsfall, Howorth, Huggeford, Hulse, Loyd, Roper, Smythe, Wilfoord, Wimberley
2. Allen, Amerex, Americe, Anguilla, Arguilla, Brain, Tresham.
3. Acheley, Adcane, Akarys, Akers, Akeris, Akiris, Akyris, Alder, Alred, Auverquerque, Belmour, Betenson, Chaderton, Collins, Conway, Cooke, Corry, Cress, Cresse, Croste, Cruden, Cyfer, Douglas, Fettiplace, Forsan, Fotheringham, Greenway, Griffinhoofe, Hall, Ingram, Keene, Le Despencer, Leslie, Lesly, Lesslie, Mileham, Montagu, Norton, Oldaker, Pawson, Pemberton, Raikes, Ramsay, Reay, Roberts, Rogers, Stafford, Stevenson, Steward, Stewart, Stringer, Tempest, Trapnell, Watkens, Westripp.
4. Betson, Bitson, Docker, Fenis, Kent, Slack, Troubridge, Vampage.
5. Barrett, Barrott, Crespine, Crespin, Crispin, Lennard, Lownes.
6. Alderson, Arabin, Brayne, Brownhill, Bruce, Holbeck, Holbecke.
7. Cathcart, Clater, Elliot, Elliott, Kernaby, Knows, Lees, Losh, Napier, Robertson, Schaw-Cathcart, Sommerville, Somervil, Smellie.
8. Clark, Clerk, Merceir, Murray, Pennycoock, Pennycuick, Rattray.
9. Andsdale, Ansdell, Basier, Basire, Bonekill, Childers-Walbanke, Cleeve, Clive, Colquhoun, Garscadden, Skirvin.
10. Crowhall, Donaldson, Garroway, MacDonald, MacDonell, M'Donnell.
11. Duncombe, Fresh, Seward, Skiddy.
12. Balfour, Boswell, Brabon; Brabourne, Craufuird, Crawford, Crawfurd, Drum-

PLATE 38—*continued.*

mond, Falconer, Goulding, Kennedy, Kirton, Watt, Weddell.
13. Audley, Bewley, Everard, Whalley, Martin.
14. Golborn, Golborne, Sotherton.
15. Edwards.

PLATE 39.

1. Billings, Brisac, Butler, Chenell, Clough-Butler, Coats, Cotes, Drewell, Gillan, Gilland, Karrick, Karricke, Keogh, Pargiter, Wolmer.
2. Bestney, Connocke, Coppin, Kemeys, Lane, Lucas, Page, Powell, Rowles, Royden, Roydon, Stone, Vidler.
3. Bethune, Fren, Frene, Healy.
4. Binks, Crofton.
5. Armit, Armitt, Arnet, Bindon, Ditford, Hallam, Oxcliffe.
6. Armstrong, Bigbery, Bygbery, Rumford.
7. Chirbrond, Dickson, Douglas, Driver, Duff, Fitz-Walter, Flynt, Forbes, Goddin, Landeth, Londeth, Mayne, Peake, Pringle, Samby.
8. Charley, Charnley, Jennins, Jupp, Lealy.
9. Allan, Anderson, Burcetre, Chivers, Maundefield, Oswald.
10. Clarke, Conyers, Coyners, Goodlad, Holland, Mackworth, Petoe, Simons, Wyrley.
11. Clapp, Fisher, Pike.
12. Clay, Claye, Cley.
13. Cusacke, Durward.
14. Ardis, Dunbar, Everingham, Grierson, Maddocks, Primrose, Rolesley, Roscruge, Rowlesley, Scot, Skippe, Tudway, Wise.
15. Duval, Duvall, Fahy, Salmond.

PLATE 40.

1. Lyndsey.
2. Lysle, Lysley.
3. Lutterford.
4. Cunninghame, Fithier, Hoggeson, Kay, Lyal, Lyall, Lyell, Mauder, Milne, Mylne, Newman, Pilmuire, Randill, Snigg, Snigge.
5. Lynne.
6. Lusher.
7. Murray.
8. Lydal, Lyddall.
9. Hill, Kyrrelorde, Lucas.
10. Knowsley, Mileson, Millsom, Stillingfleet.
11. Kynnerton.
12. Knipe, Thurstone.
13. Kington.
14. Kynaston-Edwards, Kynaston.
15. Kimpton.

PLATE 41.

1. Anderson, Auforus, Beeby, Boyd, Doughty, Dune, Fenkell, Garrick, Gowler, Groze, Innes, Le Barreu, M'Millan, Mello, Murray, Paterson, Trubshaw, Vigurs, Wegg.
2. Anstruther, Brember, Chartnay, Chartney, Fitz-Osborn, Handy, Tolman, Watford, Wright.
3. Affleck, Auchinleck.
4. Biggar, Bigger, Chambers, Graham, Haughton, Home, Paterson, Peusay, Puxty, Tweddell, Wilkinson.
5. Avison, Birney, Brecknock, Brecknoy, Burmey, Forbes, Lill, Losack.
6. Baighton, Beckford, Mercer, Starkey.
7. Beekenshall, Conolly, Cooper, Couper, Græme, Graham, Haveland, Krog, Kroge, Luttrell, Moncur, Purefoy, Pureferoy, Skeen.
8. Bowyer, Coutts, Millar, Miller, Mollington.
9. Cuningham, Essington, Grislay.
10. Belfarge, Belfrage, Degge, Dighton, Kirkland, Kirkeland, Lownde, Nanfant, Rivington, Skynner, Willyams.
11. Dun.
12. Chambley, Chambly, Layland, Spearing, Vanort.
13. Bergaigne, Bergaine, Bowrie, Clough, Dempster, Duff, Farquharson, Gundry, Kuckfield, M'Dowal, M'Duff, M'Farquhar, Milligan, Milliken, Pakington, Pender, Sapcot, Shaw, Sworder, Watlington, Young.
14. Elphingston.
15. Billingham, Lodge, Marryatt, Meyer, Penfold, Shirreff, Worthom.

PLATE 42.

1. Butler, Buttler, Crocker, Drew, Durward, Dyrwarne, Dyrrwarne, Fitz-Barnard, Forsyth, Goodale, Goodalle, Hookham, Weatherall, Wilshere.
2. Ascough, Askew, Ayscough, Aysscough, Charter, Chater, Keymer.
3. Avery, Cressall, Gentill, Harborne, Isaacson, Topping.
4. Addis, Ades, Adis, Arras, Beversham, Bottomley, Boyce, Burrish, Ciddercwe, Cledcrow, Clitherow, Harley, Higgans, Higgens, Hyatt, M'Namard, Middle-

PLATE 42—*continued.*

ton, Rothery, Treacy, Verdon, Whiteway.

5. Adam, Ambridge, Brine, Coe, Jugler, Whitelocke, Whiteley, Whitelie.
6. Adair.
7. Amenton, Banbury, Bandbury, Cassel, Cassell, Chapman, Drummond, Low.
8. Banworth, Bishop, Bisshopp, Colls, Greenfield, Jay, Mackmoragh, Macmore, Moriarty, Preston.
9. Boyle, Camp, Campe.
10. Cardwell, Dengayne, Engaine, M'Clure, Marlyn, Morris, Orton, Ortun, Stock, Winziet.
11. Aines, Ainge, Ainger, Aitken, Aitkin, Atkin, Atkins, Colston.
12. Capell, Catesnelboge, Drakenford, Drysdale, City of Edinburgh, Elliot, Elliott, Ferrie, Fisher, Gray, Grey, Groat, Hepburn, Kyle, Leckie, Litster, Loghlin, O'Loghlin, Poulton, Schindler, Scot, Stedman, Wickliffe.
13. Brassey, Colt, Devoike, Edmerston, M'Culloch, Mackenzie-Muir, Main, Prouze, Smart, Winder, Yeoman.
14. Allerton, Barry, Burr, Craig, Darcye, De Placetes, Dunk, Rokwood, Starling, Wallace.
15. Cotterall, Cotterell, Cotterill, Dunbar, Grove, Inge, Lambert.

PLATE 43.

1. Acheson, Benley, Bensley, Bensly, Boag, Bog, Bogg, Cleather, Cooper, Ekington, Ekinton, Forbes, Houston, Houston-Blakiston, Woodstock.
2. Abrey, Craig, Estrange, Jessope, Jessopp, Jessup, Thwaites.
3. Achany, Achanny, Ahany, Carse, Carss, Delaleigh, Delegh, Galaad, Hannay, Hanney, Kennan, Sermon.
4. Baker, Byrne, Byrn, Casey, Cochran, Cochrane, Lark, Larke, Neville, Trusbut.
5. Baldock, Ernst, Kinloch, Monro, Monteith.
6. Andrew, Andrews, Balfour, Brenchley, Dobbin, Fane, Killegroue, Killigroue, Maccartney, Ness, Tansley.
7. Callow, Durrant, Hanmer, Harcourt, Hurley, Oxley, Sorrell, Wallington.
8. Calston, Ewing, Haulton, Lewen, Pitcairn.
9. Calverley, Calveley.
10. Pether, Rushbrooke, Schaw, Sparrow, Stowers, Timins, Thomson, Waringe.
11. Belches, Belsches, Berington, Blayne, Cooke, Creasy, Foote, Garvey, Gell, Grandvell, Halford, Hamilton, Heathfield, Holford, Hunter, Jackson, Jermyn, Johnson, M'George, Mager, Major, Morton, Muckleston, Tayler, Walker.
12. Cholwich, Cholwick, Coulton, Danmare, Hugford, Leversey, Levesey, Mawer.
13. Barberie, Barberrie, Billam, Cantilon, Elliot, Elliott, Hawberke, Holand, Joy, See, Stair, Young.
14. Ap-Eynions, Egerton, Fourbins, Hanly, Irving, Keen, Spiers, Thomas, Wiles, Wilton, Worsycke.
15. Cox, Delaland, Desland, Dowker, Edmunds, Steuart, Stewart.

PLATE 44.

1. Aillen, Apilston, Arthur, Chandler, Coulson, Cullen, Foot, Fotheringham, Gibsone, Gotobed, Gyles, Lakington, Lapington, Lemmon, Lumley, Lumley-Saville, M'Inroy, Mansuer, Mausuen, Melhuish, Norris, Osborne, Packer, Pateson, Patison, Pattison, Playfair, Pollen, Pollener, Pulleine, Pullen, Pulleyn, Reid, Rosier, Rudge, Steuart, Stewart, Stuart, Throughston, Thruxton, Thurgryn, Thweng, Tyldesley, Woodcock, Wright.
2. Adlam, Aird, Alderington, Aldrington, Alewington, Ayton, Connor, Hawker, Horn, Horne, M'Adam, Whelpdale.
3. Aeth, Bround, Brounde, Massam, Spooner-Lillingston, Wills-Sandford.
4. Barnes.
5. Barker, Barnack, Barnake, Carrol, Carroll, Heritage, Hurd.
6. Barlay, Barley.
7. Capsal, Copland, Copeland, Coppland, Cowpland, Kennedy.
8. Aldridge, Aldrige, Anderson, Bingley, Brander, Calderwood, Christie, Cooper, Courtis, Craufurd, Crawford, Eddington, Fenwick, Fennwick, Fitz-William, Fraser, Gostling, Graham, Grierson, Heur, Hever, Ingram, Iremonger, Ironmonger, Jercy, Jersey, Johnston, Kennaway, Needham, M'Gill, Mackreth, Mackwilliams, MacLeod, Maule, Mitchell, Moll, Mort, Mow, Needham, Phin, Plumbtree, Plumpton, Plumtre, Plumtree, Radley, Redcomyn, Robertson, Russel, Russell, Seymour, Shaw, Sinclair, Snodgrass, St. Clair, St. Clair-Erskine, Stewart, Theobald, Timbrell, Toft, Tofte, Townsend, Trice, Verney, Wingrove.
9. Armistead, Auchmuty, Caswell, Combes, Cuthbert, Dancer, Dymock, Dymoke, Fearguson, Ferguson, Forster, Foster, Gilbert, Heley, Helly, Kemble, Mackenay, Makareth, Makeroth, Michel, Montgomery, Palmer, Smyth, Thompson.
10. Crawford, Evelick, Lindsay, Stacey.
11. Eggerly.
12. Braham, Brigham, Burke, Cardew, Clere, Dabridgcourt, Dellabere, Hakeliott, Harrison, Holland, Le Bon, Lewys, Marvel, Ouldsworth, Pauncefote, Peverell, Plum, Plume, Posingworth, Possingworth, Posyngworth, Scales, Scroope,

PLATE 44—*continued.*

Smyth, Swertchoff, Tatham, Walgrave, Willet, Willett, Wrangham.
13. Ainlie, Ainslie, Barnewell.
14. Delane, Stevens, Waterlow.
15. Adger, Swabey, Swaby, Usher.

PLATE 45.

1. Allen, Arther, Arthur, Auston, Barnes, Gib, Harries, Irwin, Irwine, Latouche, Rowley, Sawers, Shiels, Wenard, Wenward, Wragg.
2. Barkesworth, Barksworth, Burbridge, Ewbank.
3. Broun, Brown, Meldrum, Milne, Mosman, Mossman, Mylne, Park, Sibbald.
4. Carnie, Constable, Hoyland, Kilby, Lorimer.
5. Anne, Carey, Cary, Carmichael, Griffin, Griffith, Kepping, Mowbray, Rudd, Savage, Tanfield, Tansfield.
6. Carpenter, Depham, Donelly, Donnelly, Kirk, Monkhouse, Wandesford, Wandford.
7. Alden, Aldon, Beach, Beacher, Becher, Bruse, Bruskett, Bunford, Chetwode, Churchill, Churchman, Clarke, Clavering, Cowley, Darley, Dunsbord, Francis, Hemming, Holland, Hollond, Hughes, Jones, Kinchant, King, Long, Longfield, Maberley, Maberly, Millburn, Mirrie, Mirry, Molloy, elson, Nichols, Orpsen, Oulton, Philipse, Sparkes, Spence, Sutton, Walshe, Warrand.
8. Leche.
9. Anton, Bennett, Boles, Davidson, De Mardeston, Hargil, Hawes, Kelleher, Keteridge, Neilson, Newdich, Newdick, Newell, Notely, Osborn, Page, Penniman, Price, Senton, Simeon, Wotton.
10. Cogger, Ellisworth.
11. Ellard, Gowland, Manduit, Mandut, Manduyt, Oram, Scatchard.
12. Elliot, Elliott, Gordon, Mather, Tarell.
13. Carstairs.
14. Alleyn, Bromewich, Bromwich, Carington, Carleton, Carrington, Carryngton, Charlton, Deeves, Gale, How, Hughes, Hulleys. Hullies, Lloyd, Nosworth, Perkins, Preston, Richardson, Ritchie, Smith, Smyth, Sparrow, Tregore, Tregour, Wentworth.
15. Bates, Carrick, Erskine, Leash, Maitland.

PLATE 46.

1. Barclay, Foot.
2. Chilcote, Chilcott, Robinson.
3. Carruthers.
4. Davies, Pratter.
5. Carey, Hamlyn, Killicke, Lachlan, Lindsay, Magawley, Shee, Sinnott, Strattle, Wemyts.
6. Arundel, Arundell, Ashfield, Ashurst, Batt, Blunt, Coplestone, Crolly, Darell, Davis, Dodingsells, Doolman, Gawdy, Gravatt, Gun, Gwyer, Hayes, Holland, Huband, Jacob, Lawley, Leight, Linch, Lovet, Lovett, Low, Lowe, Odingsell, Odingsells, Owen, Perriman, Perryman, Reskinner, Travers, Trelawney, Tytherley, Westmoreland, Yonge.
7. Angellis, Angles, Caston, Dighton, Ellington, Fokke, Forty, Gibon, Gybons, Homer, King-Duckworth, Matthews, Newling, Noble, Payne.
8. Bish, Byshe, Davies, Rishton, Rushton.
9. Dawn, Dawne, Miall.
10. Crawford, Dealtry, Frances, Francies, Fraunceis, Fraunces, Frannceys, Grymes.
11. Deaken, Deakin, Hengrave, Putt, St Philibert.
12. Albrecht, Albreght, Clifford, Dean, Deane, Deram, Entwisle, Gilbert, Graham, Kenton, M'Donell, Macdonell, M'Donnell, M'Maught, Wigram.
13. Apsey, Elliot, Puget, Shand.
14. Elliot, Elliott, M'Crummen.
15. Bokenham, Du Coin, Elliston, Marmaduke, Tuck.

PLATE 47.

1. Calder.
2. Calcraft.
3. Caldwell, Cauldwell, Kadwell.
4. Call.
5. Withie.
6. Cambell, Campbell, Charlton, Covert, Hatch, Kelwich.
7. Clepole, Danvers, Fenton, Wardor.
8. Daniel.
9. Darby.
10. Elliot, Elliott.
11. Dare.
12. Ellis.
13. Darker, Peck.
14. Browne, Egerton, Murray, Scrymzeor.
15. Braimor, Edmonds, Holt, Johnston, Taylor.

PLATE 48.

1. Aiton, Flemyng, Flemynge, Fresell, Fresill, Girdler, Hamelen, Hamelin, Hamelyn, Hamlyng, Hardman, London, Ross, Tilson.

PLATE 48—*continued.*

2. Abercorne, Adams, Argyll, Asheton, Ashton, Assheton, Baillie, Bairnsfather, Baker, Barnesfather, Barton, Basset, Bassett, Blair, Booth, Borton, Bradley, Brodley, Brokesby, Cambell, Campbell, Clipsham, Cruikshanks, Cunningham, Downing, Eel, Faulks, Foulkes, French, Gabell, Gordon, Gough, Grant, Grobham, Haliday, Halliday, Herring, Humphrees, Humphreys, Ingleby, Innes, Innis, Jones, Jordon, Kercy, Kersey, Lawless, Lloyd, Lungsford, Luxford, Lychfield, M'Evers, MacGan, Macguffie, M'Iver, Magan, Norcop, Oglander, Peshall, Peter, Peters, Phillips, Rodney, Sandford, Seaton, Seton, Sheils, Shiels, Smineen, Sminfen, Stewart, Stirling, Tallerton, Tasker, Tennent, Thimbleby, Thin, Tyzard, Urquhart, Vaughan, Vennor, Vernor, Warcop, Warcup, Warcupp, Whyt, Whyting, Williams, Winstanton, Wrotesley, Wyatt, Wynn, Young.

3 Cruck, Elphingston, Ford, Galaad, Gay, Green, Jaupin, Kyneston, Riddell, Younge.

4. Abercromby, Abercrombie, Anketell, Anlaby, Basnet, Berenger, Bosom, Bosome, Bossum, Chambers, Forrest, Fox, France, Garrioch, Hanlaby, Harries, Hewlett, Hooley, Mowat, Stroode, Thom, Thornhill, Wood.

5. Anneles, Atmore, Attemore, Biron, Bonham, Breuer, Brewer, Bruer, Brumherd, Bryn, Bryne, Byron, Challon, Chiswell, Cuillen, Cusake, Ellice, Glasse, Ellis, Enell, Foster, Garnish, Garnyl, Glass, Golever, Hastings, Kinloch, Lauzon, Leicester, M'Nair, M'Nayr, Marbury, Mason, Meare, Merbury, Mere, Meres, Meyres, Metley, Minett, More, Moultrie, Moutry, Murray, Obyrne, O'Bryne, Rutherford, Rutherfurd, Skeffingham, Skeffington, Skevington, Skiffington, Sleford, Wallop, Wallopi, Warburton.

6. Acheley, Ackworth, Acworth, Adams, Allen, Aveline, Baird, Ballard, Bannatyne, Barton, Baynton, Bayntun-Rolt, Beardmore, Benton, Bervy, Best, Beynton, Biggs, Blesbie, Blesby, Bligh, Blythe, Bowles, Braynton, Brettle, Brown, Browne, Bryce, Burgess, Bury, Carkettle, Cay, Chaplin, Clark, Copley, Cotton, Cudmore, Cumby, Cure, D'aeth, Dangerfield, Dashwood, Dean, Deane, Dermott, Dimsdale, Ednor, Fettyplace, Forbes, Fotheringham, Gardener, Gardiner, Gardner, Godsal, Godsale, Godsall, Godsell, Gouch, Greenlogh, Greenway, Griffeth, Hall, Hanham, Hard, Harrison, Hughes, Jackman, Johnston, Kadrohard, Kay, Keightley, Kelshaw, Kennicot, King-Dashwood, Kumerson, Lansley, Lasley, Lawrence, Leslie, Lesly, Line, Linton, Lyne, M'Iver, Manfield, Mansfield, Micklethwaite, Milborne, Mileham, Miles, Moulden, Mucklewaite, Nalder, Neal, Neale, Newbold, Nicklin, Patten, Pemberton, Phetoplace, Raikes, Raparils, Reade, Reading, Reay, Reeve, Reynolds, Richards, Ricroft, Riding, Rosington, Rossington, Roycroft, Ryan, Rycroft, Ryecroft, Sharp, Sinclair, Sissons, South, Stanley, Stirlin, Stump, Sutton, Sybsey, Taber, Tempest, Tilney, Todrick, Treacher, Trentham, Troyhin, Tyas, Tyes, Vaux, Waldo, Waldoc, Walsh, Walsh-Benn, Walshe, Ward, Watkins, Waynflete, Welsh, West, White, Whitwell, Willard, Willock, Winde, Wybergh.

7. Andrewes, Andrews, Annesley, Den, Dena, Main, Mair, Tanner.

8. Auncell, Beaton, Beaumont, Beton, Betton, Betune, Booth, Boothe, Borrett, Bowdon-Butler, Bramhall, Brant, Brett, Brewes, Brews, Brewse, Bromhall, Brooks, Brown, Bruce, Bryden, Clement, Copeland, Coryton, Coxhead, Crook, Depham, Escot, Escot, Evans, Fairfax, Fitzpaine, Garrittee, Goode, Grace, Greseley, Grestey, Griffith, Hagerston, Halkett, Herle, Hustwick, Kelton, Kendall, Ketland, Loterel, M'Clintock, M'Lintock, Maddock, Maurice, Muckle, Noble, Paynell, Phitton, Rawston, Rawstorne, Richards, Rishton, Rome, Seabright, Sebright, Sheath, Slingsby, Staple, Sterling, Stirling, Strange, Strangewayes, Strangeways, Strangways, Strangewiche, Surtees, Taylor, Turner, Underwood, Urswicke, Wake, Walpole, Wrangham, Yenn.

9. Ailsa, Arnold, Askeam, Askeham, Askham, Bertwhistle, Brown, Byrtwhysell, Carminow, Carmynow, Carmenow, Casaer, Ceasser, Colston, Coulson, Coulston, Courtenay, Delves, Durham, Fawcet, Ffrench, Freer, French, Godolphin, Grierson, Gwynne, Harflete, Harfett, Henraghty, Izzard, James, Kennedy, Kingdom, Mackmaure, Mallam, Metge, Monypenny, Nedham, Nutter, Orme, Pugh, Raitt, Reardon, Remnant, Rimmer, Ryton, Sargant, Septuans, Sergeant, Shone, Simmons, Solay, Soley, Symonds, Symmonds, Weyland, Young.

10. Alvas, Alves, Auste, Barney, Barns, Barron, Bell, Berney, Blair, Blagnier, Bouling, Bowly, Burket, Burkett, Catcher, Cheap, Chelsum, Cholmeley, Cholmondeley, Crawford, Cumine, Cuming, Cummin, Cumming, Dale, Danson, Darby, Darley, De Blaguiere, Derby, Dolman, Donald, Donaldson, Ellis, Este, Falknor, Ferrier, Field, Foller, Folvill, Fovell, Gilliot, Girle, Goldie, Golding, Goudie, Gouldie, Greenville, Gregor, Gregorie, Grenville, Gwatkin, Hamley, Harrower, Heathfield, Hesketh, Heskett, Hiders, James, Joseph, Kelso, Kiltie, Kelty, Lawson, Leke, Lovell, M'Laws, Maltby, Merefield, Michael, Miln, Milnes, Mitchall, Mitchell, Modyford, Molineux, Oatly, Ottley, Paul, Paule, Peterborough, Phillips, Platt, Price, Randoll, Rede, Reed, Reede, Reid, Roby, Routledge, Rowan, Rowand, Sandpach, Scrambler, Sicklemore, Skeen, Spilsbury, Spurwaye, Spyer, Spyre, Stephenson, Stevens, Stevenson, Stevynson, Tippet, Vallance,

PLATE 48—*continued.*

Vanderplank, Warnford, Watur, Wauchop, Whitefoord, Widdrington, White, Winton, Youl.

11. Acheson, Anwit, Auchterlonie, Aughterlony, Barne, Bedingfield, Benge, Blesset, Blesset, Brendon, Broadbelt, Brograve, Brotherton, Brown, Browne, Bussie, Bytheses, Cavenish-Browne, Chancelor, Chancellor, Cheslie, Cheureuse, Chiesly, Chislie, Cole, Copwood, Cornish, Cotton, Crombie, Crook, Crumb, Cullen, Cussons, Cuttes, Davies-Bowen, De Beauvoir, De Visme, Dingwall, Dixon, Dobbie, Dobie, Drake, Dumbleton, Edwards, Englefield, Ernley, Ernly, Ethelstan, Ewerby, Fenner, Fielding, Forbes, Fordyce-Dingwall, Fox, Francis, Fraser, Gambier, Garshore, Gartshore, Gasselyn, Gasselyne, Gent, Godfrey, Goodall, Greaves, Guyot, Hapsburgh, Harris, Hereford, Jeppe, Kendall, Lightborne, Lightbourne, Lye, Martin, Martyn, Mather, Matthew-Mawbey, Messer, Messing, Monro, Morby, Morris, Moselay, Moseley, Mosly, Mossey, Noble, Nove, Ochterlonie, Odehull, Odell, Ouchterlony, Page, Parminter, Pattle, Paxton, Phillimore, Piessf, Pilford, Pinney, Poulain, Purton, Ramsay, Ramson, Raymond, Read, Reade, Reath, Reeves, Remnant, Rofey, Rofy, Rogers, Ross, Rothschild, Salt, Sandilands, Saumarez, Scopholme, Sloan, Souchay, Speccott, Stannard, Strong, Stronge, Struthers, Tickel, Tickell, Torphicen, Tovey, Turberville, Venner, Venour, Wadman, Wags, Way, Webb, Whetham, Wilberforce, Wild, Williams, Wilson, Wishart, Wylde, Wynn-Williams, Wynne.

12. Agard, Bilson, Billson, Burt, Corney, Curl, Currell, Daunt, Goatham, Grenehalgh, Haggarth, Hollings, Horn, Hunt, Hunter, Langhorn, Langhorne, Logan, Lothian, Louthian, Newport, Pierie, Povey, Sclater, Sherd, Wait, Waite, Waith, Wayte, Whetstone.

13. Austin, Beawfice, Bogie, Boggie, Davie, Dewar, Dowdal, Dowdall, Evans, Farrington, Lamb, Langholme, Llewellyn, Lluellin, Malmains, Normand, Parry, Pascol, Price, Richards, Rowe, Stopford.

14. Albalanda, Arderne, Bacon, Barron, Bellew, Bleddyn, Bleeddyn, Bodkin, Boscawen, Boscowen, Calton, Cantlow, Clotworthy, Craige, Craigg, Craigge, Craigie, Craigy, Crewe, Crudington, Eastwood, Euston, Findlay, Findley, Fitz-Gerald, Fitzgerald, Gairden, Gaisford, Gammon, Garden, Georges, Guinness, Hammond, Harper, Huddersfield, Jeffcott, Jephcott, Keogh, Langley, Legryle, Lisbone, Lisborne, Magenis, Maginnise, Nisbet, Nisbett, Orpwood, Phillipson, Quaplod, Rollo, Sandom, Sidney, Swinny, Trotter, Vere, Ware, Wildbore.

15. Albeney, Alberry, Aderson, Allsop, Allsup, Alsope, Allardice, Allen, Ardington, Arthington, Baldwin, Barclay, Blanckagam, Blantyre, Bradston, Brander, Brasier, Brazier, Brummel, Brummell, Buchanan, Campbell, Clayton, Cooper, Creed, Dabetot, Dabitot, Daniels, Davy, Duffield, Duguid, Dwigwid, Edwards, Fairholm, Forbes-Leith, Foscott, Foxcote, Foulis, Fowlis, Francis, Gairdner, Garioch, Golbourn, Goodwright, Gordon, Goulburn, Grayhurst, Gypses, Hall, Higgs, Higgan, Hill, Hodgson, Hopkin, Ireland, Irwin, Jessop, Jolly, Kennison, Laing, Lang, Law, Learmonth, Leathes, Leith, Lemoine, Makepiece, Marshall, Morant, Morland, Mower, Murray, Mussenden, Newmarch, Newsham, Newville, Omer, Paytherus, Pearson, Petrie, Phaire, Pigott, Porteous, Prior, Rathbone, Rest, Revett, Rubridge, Salt, Sand, Scarisbrick, Shanan, Shand, Sinclair, Southcomb, St. Clair, Tattersall, Towle, Travess, Trimmer, Turvile, Wade, Waldie, Walker, Walkingshaw, Walters, Ward, Whannell, Whittington, Wirgman.

PLATE 49.

1. Abberbury, Aberbury.
2. Abercrombie, Ardem, Ardyn, Barbour, Bogley, Bruges, Christie, De Bruges, Spurrier, St. John, Welch, Whitford.
3. Abernethy, Bowring, Dunnage, Evre, Froggat, Froggatt, Knoell, Knoll, Knolle, Knowles, M'Ilwham, Rennie.
4. Areskine, Ballantyne, Ballentine, Bannatyne, Erskine, Feyry, Gladstanes, Glaidstanes, Gledstanes, Parkhurst, Treves.
5. Alexander, Beaver, Beevor, Beynham, Brooks, Brookes, Coram, Corham, Eaton, Howel, Howell, M'Lagan, Molineux, Sadleyr, Symcock, Symcot, Symcott, Trowell.
6. Binning, Herrington, Hingham, Horsley, Magawley, Mawgawley, Weldy.
7. Beckman, Bunn, Martyr.
8. Aiken, Caldwell, Houndegart, Leg, Legg, Thornton, Whittlebury.
9. Beriffe, Cadman, Gibson.
10. Ashenden, Chester, Constantine, Dagworth, Julien, Maugham, Maughan, Uffleet, Ufflet.
11. Brews, Brewse, Colvil, Colville, Dalby, Dible, Dibley, Grant, Helard, Hellard.
12. Crosbie, Crosbey, Dall, Eastoft, Edgar, Habgood, Leir, Smith, Young.
13. Brandwood, Corp, Darby, Durand, Easton, Faconbridge, Hexman, M'Millan, Meredyth, Seamark, Sparrow, Stelton, Uhthoff, Wale.
14. Blunden, Holmes, Lewis, Marley, St. Pere, St. Pierre, Sent-Pier.
15. Eddowes.

PLATE 50.

1. Alfrey, Allfrey, Hogan, Manfield.
2.
3. Alison, Dexter, Garman, Garmon.
4. Baskenford, Baskin, Glendenning, Knyvett, Somery.
5. Barsane, Bartane, Barton, Fasant, Huet, Macbride, Norreys, Norris, Parvise.
6. Barwick, Ellard, Neale, Stapley, Williams.
7. Case, Casse, Schomberg.
8. Bean, Beane, Cashall, Hervey, Morse, Ogilvie, Rees.
9. Bourne, Carver, Ilam, Ilamy, Stedman.
10. Avenet, Avenett, Bowdan, Bowden, Delahay, Jacques, Wardon.
11. De Gray, Hobbs, Lawford, Sinclair, Thorp, Truscoat, Truscott.
12. Delapipe.
13. Abbot, Elrick, Allen, Bayley, Chalkhill, Elrick, Hackney, Johnson, Marchant, Ogilvy, Partridge, Redman, Skelton.
14. Atwater, Ellisworth, Lillie, Wadham.
15. Denne, Escudmore, Manners, Manners-Sutton, Roos, Rosse, Ross-Lewin, Sutton.

PLATE 51.

1. Ewart, Goreley, Gorley, Greaves, Grimshaw, Ironside, Lawnde, M'Donald, Parnther, Rich.
2. Aldewinckle, Aldewincle, Aldewinkell, Aldwinckle, Aldwinkle,
3. Alexander.
4. Barrington, Burghep, Burghepe, Hevengingham, Heveringham, Paynter, Pitches.
5. Barr, Lichfield, Lychfeld.
6. Barrowman, Gordon, Hewitt, Mountjoy, Murphy.
7. Aland, Betts, Farmer, Fortescue, Gilbes, Heart, Husee, Meager, Panther.
8. Asadam, Booker, Bushby, Cassy, Horrell, Rooke.
9. Carrol, Cocks, Coxs, Den, Denne, Fulton, Horrocks.
10. Andegarvia, Anger, Aunger, Barwicke, Baxter, Breach, De Fortibus, Hellord, Highlord, Ledger, Norris.
11. Dekener, Viel, Vieler.
12. Beauford, Beaufort, Bell, Buck, Degon, Farquharson, Fencourt, Marson, Melles, Menles, Porter, Raglan, Renolds, Ryland, Somerset, Somester, Sommaster, Wilmot.
13. Coudray, Coudrey, Condry, Doran, Edwardes-Tucker, Emly, Garland, Garlant, Lowman, Marke, Pendleton, Simmonds. Simon, Smerdon, Tucker, Tuckie, Tusser,
14. Albert, Auvray, Comberton, Dorien, Elwin, Elwyn, Elwynn, Haig, Haigh, Neilson.
15. Braddyll, Cushney, Depden, Deptun, Ennis.

PLATE 52.

1. Algist, Crosby, Drewe, Druce, Moody, Moodye.
2. Alchorn, Alchorne, Douglas, Elsworth, Flood, Gamoll.
3.
4. Beckwell, Bekewell, Farrier, Ferrier, Fuller, Gawaine, Gawayne, Leaky.
5. Best, Brest, Buchanan, Budworth, Grenvile, Gwinnell.
6. Bellasis, Bellasses, Crouchfield, Crutchfield, Fenton, Somerford, Watson.
7. Bowell, Cater, Hood, Jacomb.
8. Anderson, Alston, Alstone, Bedingfeld, Bedingfield, Buckley, Cartland, Clack, Gill, Gleg, Glegge, Gourlay, Gourley, Graham, Graves, Greenaway, Hore, Kebble, Marley, Maxwell, Menzies, Purland, Reid, Sivedale, Wilcotts.
9. Carey, Carry.
10. Aynesworth, Ayneworth, Aynworth, Dornford, Irball, Johnes, Johns, Joynour, Le Scot, Shepard, Sheppard, Sheperd, Spittal, Spratt, Waddell.
11. Currey, Currie, Danheck, Dorville, Dupre.
12. Anderton, Athowe, Brasy, Cobb, Cobbes, Davernett, Dowd, Ewen, Goldsmith, Ireland, Jennings, Kelloway.
13. Espinasse, Fiennes, Haskins.
14. Dupont, Esdaile, Foord.
15. Cary, Estmerton, Fenner, Foxall, Gairden, Gardyne, Gowilie.

PLATE 53.

1. Hussey.
2. Grayson, Martham, Stanhope.
3. Bolger, Scaife.
4. Witham.
5. Grant-Macpherson, Justice, M'Combie, Mackintosh, Macpherson, Macritchie Moffat, Sutherland.
6. Conway, Custance, Dickenson, Gent, Gray, Longe, Mounehense, Sandon, Scot, Seymour, Solers.
7. Hay.
8. Bownell, Haliburton, Hallyburton, Stewart.
9. Handcock.
10. Arnold, Coplestone, Killand, Turner, Wolrich.
11. Armesbury, Cridland, Hardisty, Haulton, M'Kenzie, Payne, Strange, Wedgewood, Wescope, Westcope, Westcott, Westcot.
12. Haselfoot, Hassellfoot.
13. Avison, Byde, Halls, Loney, Partington, Reynett.
14. Hase-Lombe, Lomb.
15. Hamilton.

PLATE 54.

1. Ambler, Amerance, Annes, Anness, Annis, Ascon, Askwith, Cayle, Cayly, Hamilton, Lorimer, Neale.
2. Ansert, Macdonald, M'Dowall.
3. Alured, Alvarde, Alverd, Andre, Dilkes, Gair, Gant.
4. Benvil, Benvill, Blachford, Blackford, Blashford, Hickford, Hoppe, Isham, Malcolm, Malcom, O'Shee, Sellers.
5. Bellere, Bryson, Brysoun, Bryssan, Bryssone, Finlayson, Hardie, Saunders, Sym, Tooker, Vivian.
6. Abden, Beauchamp, Coates, Coats, Dolphin, Dunstable, Edlin, Glocester, Gloucester, O'Kerney, Wingfield.
7. Cart, Caw, Finlayson.
8. Blakeney, Butler, Cauley, Cawley, St. Leger, Sweetnam.
9. Bradstreet, Chads, Cherwood, Dench, Germin, Germyn, Makepeace, Ramsay, Rochefort, Steuart, Stewart, Stuart.
10. Drummond, Kinaird, Kinnaird, Lawrence, Mauditt, Mauduyt, Tytler.
11. Boxsted, Boxstead, Considine, Craigdallie, Crean, Crosse, Dowler, Durham.
12. Bone, Boun, Bounn, Burgin, Dunbar, Heald, Johnson, Terell.
13. Abeleyn, Aberbuthnet, Allison, Arbuthnot, Banester, Bartelott, Beck, Charnell, Douglas, Vicarey, Vicary, Vikary, Yeo.
14. Archdale, Archdell, Barker, Bausefield, Bowles, Bray, Braye, Cotsford, Estercombe, Furbisher, Gilbert, Grigson, Jenks, Johnson, Lascells, Laward, Laware, Lawarre, Leslie, Stone, Malet, Mallet, Meredith, Palmer, Pinkney, Plaisto, Plaistow, Playstow, Plomsted, Pole, Poole, Reeves, Stanier, Tellau, Thomlinson, Tillard, Tomlinson, Tylney, Unett, Warre, West, Williamson.
15. Bowes, Brakedall, Cawdor, Cole, Crow, D'Eureux, Doane, Done, Donne, Egerton, Eureux, Hardel, Hardell, Irvine, Kettle, Lyndon, Ould, Segrave.

PLATE 55.

1. Anleby, Anselby, Anselbie, Charlewood, Gilder, Marshall.
2. Anncell, Auncell, Gordon, Hext, Heysham, Hoare, Lingard, Plonckett, Plonket, Plonkett, Southy.
3.
4. Freeth, Horwood, Knight, Oxenbridge.
5. Pattison.
6. Anvory, Arpin, Bellis, Irvine, Mausted.
7. Butts, Foquett, Hall, Horsey, Horsman, M'Laughlan.
8. Dowdeswell, Watson.
9. Cayle, Colvil, Colville, Spring.
10. Dessen, Dychfield, Fyler, Grilles, Grylls, Penny, Philpot, Prestage, Prestwick, Prestwich, Speke.
11. Duxbury.
12. Bidlake.
13. Burn, Burne, Dingwall, Douglas, Enswell, Entwissell, Gray, Harte, Pringle.
14. Binns, Esse, Hesketh, Macklellan, M'Lagan, M'Laren, M'Lellan, Plompton Price, Sublet.
15. Blanchard, Everest, Govan, Kavanagh, Taap, Tapp.

PLATE 56.

1. Cheeke, Claus, Deans, Haselerton, Hone, Nixon, Oxborough, Oxburgh, Reddingfield.
2. Barnard, Barnett.
3. Berger, Chrystie, Crab, Crabbe, Deaves, L'Estrange, MacDougall, M'Dougall, M'Dowall, M'Dowell, M'Owl, Madox.
4. Boon, Boone, Brodie, De Brevill, Keegan, Kendall, Leder, Macpharlane, M'Pharlin, Samborne, Vardon, Winford.
5. De Chandew, Drummond, Fontain, Fontaine, Knevet, Poynten.
6. Bisset, Cormick, De Den, De Dena, Tipper.
7. Carvelt, Carwell, Cosgrave, Dawson, Kekewich, Lade, Leversage, Little, M'Gie, Pater, Poultney, Pultney, Stonard, Thornton, Traves.
8. Beal, Beall, Ebsworth, Elmslie.
9. Abbeford.
10. Arkell, Arkle, Elphingston, Floyd, Hughes, Laurence, Lawrence, Reading, Reding.
11. Anderson.
12. Mortlake.
13. Amerle, Aumarle, Aumerle, Colshull, Coytmore, Elwell, Hancock, Hancox, Honeyman, Honyman, Hounyman, Romaine, Srabonne.
14. Brander, Cobb, Concanon, Crooks, De Betum, Foster, Fountaine, Knollis, Knollys, Knowles, Laws, Luff, Mackinder, M'Kinder, Mascall, Oliphant, Packington, Pakington, Sarmon, Smith, Strafford.
15. Bevis, Bickenor, Bicknor, Bykenore, Brumfield, Ely, Feast, Fletcher, Quin, Savage, Stock, Wiglesworth.

PLATE 57.

1. Attwood, Cunningham, Everit, Everitt, Govesy, Lovetoft, Lovetot, Moberly, Modburley, Moderley, Rodger.
2. Ashawe.
3. Everet, Everett.
4. Merrilees.
5. Andrewes, Andrews.
6. Cheyn, Cheyne, De Bryan, Dennett, Duff, Fromond, Fromont, Gilles, Gow, Hagarty, Johnston, Jopling, Joppling,

PLATE 57—*continued.*

Lowther, Nottingham, Pape, Wichingham, Witchingham.
7. Brough, Cossars, Delaney, Godeston, Graden, Grindlay, Grindley, Hatfield, Fenchman, Hunter, Knesworth, Kneysworth, Love, MacLeod, Proud, Smythe, Storks.
8. Exeter, Knapton.
9. Dewell, Dewelle, Hearn, Hearne, Prosser, Snowden, Stone.
10. Denham, Foss, Merrey, Southam, Steuart, Stewart.
11. Fairford.
12. Douglas, Erwin.
13. Anglesey, Biddell, Biddle, Biddelle, Dowley.
14. Bowdon, Eve, Farington, Fox, Gilberd, Gunn, Hackvill, Holland, Ram.
15. Dove.

PLATE 58.

1. Hall.
2. Halfhead.
3. Glover, Hallman, Halman.
4. Macarty.
5. M'Beth.
6. M'Carlie, M'Kerlie.
7. Bretargh, Fowkroy, Nanby.
8. Nanfant, Ponpons.
9. Anderson, Bentley, Merick, Nanfant, Nanphan, Stone.
10. Oakden, Wolferstan.
11. Hender, Ockleshaw.
12. O'Cobthaigs.
13. Bryde, Pace.
14. Packington, Pakington.
15. Broker, Brooke, De Capel, Elliot, Elliott, Page, Seaman.

PLATE 59.

1. Annandale, Bempde, Burchett, Capp, Fairholm, Johnson, Johnston, Johnstone, Johnstoun, Knight, Walden, Warton.
2. Bense, Benst, Bensted, Benstead, Norris.
3. Benham, Benhan, Bengham, Bruckshaw, Bruckshow, Cook, Holton, Kirwan.
4. Bazeley, Bazley, Drew, MacCausland, Pridham, Robb, Savory.
5. Bayloll.
6. Leigham.
7. Bennet, Bennett.
8. Lellow, Lelou, Lelow, Matson, Osbourne, Stackpoole, Wylie.
9. Barwis, Brady.
10. Harbour, Leckie, Lickie, Millan, Muirhead, Pegriz.
11. Chichester, Tuckey.
12. Bruce, Cochran, Cochrane, Darling, Davidson, Douglass, Drummond, Hamilton, Leak, Scott, Stewart, Whytt.
13. Chipchase, Chipehase, Greby, Lendon, Stretton.
14. Bardolfe, Bardolph, Butterfield, Chisholme, Clifford, Gallaway, Galloway, Ingo, Thornton, Williamson.
15. Cobben, Cobbin, Cobbyn, Cobenn, Cobyn, Ogilvie, Ogilvy.

PLATE 60.

1. Brogden, Clutterbuck, Lusy, Parsons, Wolfall.
2. Cloun, Clun.
3. Colborne, Dodds, Fiske, Flote, Harcla, Harcle, Peploe, Welley, Willey.
4. Butt, Drayner, Halton.
5. Althan, Althaun, Comrie, Comry, Giffard, Hood, M'Leurg, Roydhouse, Ruffy.
6. Booth, Bowth, Dias.
7. Arel, Arle, Bradbury, Halleweel, Halley, Hunt.
8. Bowne, Bowyn, Grimwood, Jepson, Maunell, Sweet, Timpson.
9. Boulsted, Boulstred, Bulstrode, Bulteel' Bultell, De Burg, Matthews, Neat, Pembridge.
10. Burwasch, Burwasche, Burwash, Donaldson, Saltmarsh, Saltmarshe.
11. Bucket, Field, Irvine, Jefferyes, Jeffries.
12. Burghersh.
13. Burgace, Conran, M'Kowan, Reidheugh, Rodick.
14. Brickenden, Brunsell, Bunhill, Burnell, Grubbe, Meers, Stalton, Stayiton.
15. Boxall, Boxell, Brittain, Brittaine, Jarman, Maxwell, Seymer.

PLATE 61.

1. Bell, Jeffry, Nalour, Norreys-Jackson.
2. Duff.
3. Cludde, Farnham, Moore, Moorton, More, Mountcashell, Pemberton, Varnham.
4. Norwood, Northwood.
5. Balguy, Chamber, Chambers, Legh, Milles, Polhill.
6. Henley-Ongley.
7. Biss, Glegg, Hawksmore, Lloyd, Maher, Norden, Onslow, Sandford, Sproule, White.
8. Brindley, Brinley, Herbert, Hickey, Wakeling.
9. Andrewes, Andrews, Lister, Lloyd, Rowe, Semple.
10. Borrowes, Borrows, Coe, Coo, Gordon-Taylor, Rivers, Taylor.
11. Burton.

PLATE 61—*continued.*

12. Barnes, Bolingbroke, Paulet, Pawlet.
13. Rous, Russell.
14. Cleve, Cliffe, Clive, Evelyn, Finch, Finche, Watson.
15. Townshend.

PLATE 62.

1. Ashworth, Aswell, Ashwell, Birkby, Buckby, Hakewood, Lichfield, Manson, Muston, Pilland, Wicks.
2. Arscot, Arscott.
3. Asketine, Askentine, Coats, Cotes, Dawbeney, Goldsmidt, Hammersley, Harvey, Minshall, Minshull, Mynshull, Wadeson.
4. Aldeborough, Audborough, Bottlesham, Delalynd, Delalynde, Fludyer, Garraway, Grieve, Hoke, Hooke, Hooker, St. Owen, Snape, Snepp, Storey.
5. Atkins, Atkyns, Bratt, Lysons.
6. Aylford, Aylnford, Conran, Gemell, Gemill, Gemmell.
7. Black, Francklyn, Franco, Frankland, Gibbard, Inglefield.
8. Bigg, Dempsey, Gardiner, Gardner, Lowder, Tomlins.
9. Blackburn, Chamberlen, Hastings, Staples, Wilks.
10. Aiskell, Aiskill, Askill, Bledlow, Delalynd, Gray, Homan, Kennedy, Langlands. Ufford.
11. Billing.
12. Blewet, Blewett, Blewitt, Bleuett, Sibbald Tillard.
13. Dundas, Odingsells.
14. Eure, Wilkinson, Williamson.
15.

PLATE 63.

1. Denny, Thompson, Thomson.
2. Ashmore, Aubemarle, Bromell, Hackett, Southerne.
3. Allardice, Birkes, Britten, Goslett, Inglish, Mervyn, Tinling, Woodville.
4. Ibetson.
5. Alexander, Dupre-Alexander, Row, Whetham.
6. Bulmer, Cantelow, Davies, Greham, James, Layman, Little, Moore, Purse, Sanders, Saunders, Servante, Smith.
7. Amitesly, Anelshey, Anmetesley, Annelshie, Auteshey, Antesley, Basceilly, Bebb, Dixon, Kane, Nind, Nisbet.
8. Densy, Fortune, Keane, Mallard, Northcote, Parker.
9. Aston, Atkins, Bayne, Cousmaker, Coussmaker, Dawson, Flint, Jardine, Langdale, Martaine, Martin, Martyn, Oswald, Rose, Salmon, Twiss, Vandergucht, Vivian, Wardlaw.
10. Adshead, Adshade, Aype, Beckwith, Binge, Bostock, Byfield, Caldwoodley, Carew, Chittock, Coxton, Delaney, Delany, Delatune, Edwards, Galliers, Gollop, Gort, Hamilton, Homes, Howieson, Ireby, Jameson, Joce, Kardaile, Kardoyle. Laban, Lenaghan, Maut, Sandby, Shewen Webley.
11. Scofield.
12. Aucher, Aucherr, Auchinleck, Burough Burrowes, Burrows.
13. Anvers, Barbe, Bursted, Button, Carfrae. Collier, Collyer, Croft, Crofts, Danvers. De Boys, De Winton, Dine, Dive. Drake, Hill-Trevor, Estanton, Farrington, Fitz-Waryn, Gobel, Hogg, Holerton. Inchbold, Inman, Judson, Leighton. Lowdes, Lowe, Lucas, Mabb, M'Hutcheon, Monck, Monk, Nallinghurst, Palmer, Peacock, Pearse, Penleaze, Rich, Rust, Salvin, Seton, Shorthose, Somerville, St. Barbe, Stopford, Twist, Warren, Werkesley, Werkesly, Wesley, Wilkins-Cann, Workesley, Worsley, Wyvill.
14. Barlande, Fonnereau, Mettord, Murphy Nairn, Pain, Powell.
15. Ashe, Baillie, Baird, Baker, Benger, Boucherett, Cordall, Curson, Ease, Heely, Hutchinson, Langley, Leigh, Mudge, Nugent, O'Bierne, Okes, Peacocke, Prendergast, Pressly, Twiss, Twysden.

PLATE 64.

1. Cooper, Couper, Hartopp, Wakering.
2. Wakeman.
3. Walker.
4. Walcott.
5. Amory, Arderne, Astley, Linnet, Raines, Reymes, Spitty, Waldegrave.
6. Walker.
7. Jones, Measter, Peck, Yon.
8. Massey, Yeale.
9. Young.
10. Allatt.
11. Rasdall.
12. Allen.
13. Amerdley, Gilroy.
14. Allison.
15. Amherst, Amhurst.

PLATE 65.

1. Ballard, Beauvoir, Brett, Coleridge, Crawford, De Montacute, Dysart, Goslike, Gostwick, Gostwyke, Granville, Harokins, Henvill, Hobson, Holme, J'Anson,

PLATE 65—*continued.*

Lesly, M'Call, Mansham, Marsham, Masham, Montacute, Montague, Mont-Hermer, Parnell, Peckwell, Prestwood, Scott, Selenger, Shirt, Short, Slocombe, Tinney, Wolmer.
2. Adamson, Allen, Bollen, Calton, Chere, Cheseldon, Cheseldyne, Cogan, Coggan, Forester, Forster, Fothergill, Glover, Higham, Huntley, Huntly, Marriot, Marriott, Maryet, Maryot, Moris.
3. Agbury, Boger, Cranford, Ricardo.
4. Banner, Meek.
5. Bance, Clements, Irvine, Irving, Lavie, Leach, Leache, Quintin, Randes, Trowterback.
6. Arnet, Barlow, Barrowe, Bennet, Berrie, Berry, Boddington, Boddinton, Buckworth, Clarke, Conigsby-Capel, Fletcher-Goodrich, Hare, Knell, Mapletoft, Nesham, Ravenhill, Russell, Seed, Walford, Woodcock.
7. Caning, De Newburg, Ewes, Manico, Newbury, Redford, Sealy.
8. Abingdon, Cantrell, Blyth, Cantrell, Grindal, Grindall, Gwyn, Jacobs, Mytton, Teasdale.
9. Capes, Castell, De Maderston, Deneston, Deveston, Donovan, Newbald, Newbold, Warr.
10. Burnham, Davies, Denston, Floyer, Wauch, Waugh, Williams, Witty.
11. Agall, Aggs, Cooper, D'Arcy, Lardner.
12. Blossom, Blossome, Chadwell, Dawe, Dyas, Glen, Glenn, Grigg.
13. Beseley, Katheram, Rossell.
14. Delavere, Elcock, France, Giesque, Kensing, Pukring, Roe, Yardley.
15. Booth, Brounker, Cokerell, Crampton, Elrington, Grant, Gryme, Kibble, Verdelin.

PLATE 66.

1. Algloval, Apletree, Bruyin, Bruyn, Estower, Estewer, Kemp, Worthington, Yaxley.
2. Allan.
3.
4. Abadam, Anwick, Despard, Douglas, Ferguson, King, Krowton, Remington, Scot.
5. Hammond, Manning, Morison, Morow, Morrison, Slaughter, Stevenson, Trewent.
6. Abbetot, Mace, Montchantsey, Mountchansey, Officer.
7. Bacon, Jones, Lun, Lunn, Ronaldson, Tiffin.
8. Abby, Adamson, Atcliff, Atcliffe, Atclyff, Atclyffe, Caddy, Corbreake, Crosse, Featherston, Featherstone, Fergant, Guthrie, Petrie, Scholes, Squarey, Tinker.
9. Alms, Andrew, Andrewes, Andrews, Annesley, Astrie, Astry, Aurd, Baynbridge, Baynbrigge, Beckwith, Belasis, Bellasis, Bell, Bellewe, Bellingham, Bickwith, Boorne, Boultbee, Boultree, Boyse, Bradford, Broadley, Browne, Budoxhead, Budorshide, Bulworth, Burleigh, Byrdall, Cahn, Cahun, Carling, Carr, Carre, Chaytor, Chetitor, Cheyne, Collingwood, Colquhoun, Court, Couts, Creketot, Dear, Dick, Dirom, Dixon, Doling, Dorn, Downes, Edington, Egerton, Everton, Farnham, Finlason, Forbes, Forrester, Forster, Forteath, Foster, Fouler, Franks, Fraser, Frisel, George, Goff, Goffe, Goostrey, Gordon, Green, Greene, Grimston, Gunter, Hanning, Hargrave, Hartgule, Hartgull, Hemenhall, Hill, Hislop, Hoad, Hoare, Horner, Humble, Hunter, Hutchinson, Hutchison, Jones, Karr, Keith, Ker, Kerr, Kewley, Knightley, Ladbrooke, Lea, Lee, Leybourn, Lister, Lizars, Locker, Loyd, Lyde, Lyster, M'Adam, Macadam, M'Dougall, M'Guire, Machell, M'Kimmie, Macleay, M'Leay, M'Phaill, Mason, Maxwell, Mescow, Mortimer, Mortymer, Myreson, Nell, Norcliffe, Noyes, Oakeley, O'Connell, Ord, Osbaldeston, Pain, Parker, Pawson, Peele, Peirce, Penyng, Peveleedon, Piggot, Plowden, Popham, Potkin, Power, Raikes, Raynsford, Rayson, Rede, Ridgley, Rigaud, Riggeley, Rigmaiden, Rigmayden, Robinson, Roe, Romayne, Rone, Ronne, Roper, Row, Sage, Scot, Scott, Sempill, Semple, Shepley, Simmons, Smith, Spence, Spens, Standley, Stanley, Stirling, Strachan, Threipland, Vigors, Wackett, Walker, Whitehead, Woodhead, Woodman, Wright, Wybrants, Wychcombe, Wylde, Yyles, Young, Younge.
10. Calder, Chalie, Coldstream, Donithorn, Erskine, Gobion, Lindsay, Llewellyn, Louthfuttis, Rooe, Seaton, Solley, Solly, Wagner, Walker.
11. Abergavenny, Bovile, Bovyle, Bovyll, Bragg, Bulbeck, Bulmer, Bullmer, Cardington, Clovel, Clovell, Cooper, D'Acre, Daniel, D'Arcy, Fawset, Fawsset, Hody, Hogh, Hoghton-Bold, Hoo, Houghton, Huddy, James, Longsdale, O'Daniel, Oxnam, Plesehy, Polewheele, Polwhill, Polwhele, Ridley, Sikes, Staynings, Tailboys.
12. Ball, Cant, Chardin, Charnock, Collens, Collins, Dakeham, De Cardonnel, Dilke, Dow, Dowds, Dowson, Forbes, Formby, Graham, Greensmith, Grindlay, Grindley, Gulline, Hood, Leitch, Lempriere, M'Gallock, M'Gassock, M'Guffock, Marshall, Mathews, Mitchener, Nicholls, Norbery, Norbury, O'Keefe, Peterkin, Peterkyn, Reynolds, Rous, Sinclair, Sly.
13. Aylesford, Bandenell, Beville, Blackman, Craven, Eckford, Keily, Llewellin, Napleton, Paiton, Piers, Sandys.
14. Biggs, Charlton, Cholwell, Cockrell, Covert, Crouchley, Eades, Farmer, Garton, Haseley, Hoare, Hunt, Kett, Kirkland, Leverage, M'Lachlan, Maclauchlan, Ni-

PLATE 66—*continued.*

gon, Prentis, Sarsfield, Sexton, Stephen, Terrell, Walrond.

15. Alençon, Burnell, Cooper, Cuncliffe, Delaber, Dellaber, Donelan, Donnelan, Fanshaw, Hearn, Jenner, Jenoure, Jenoyre, Jeynor, Joiner, Larkan, Larken, Lyggins, M'Laggan, Nash, Proctor, Rives, Satterthwaite, Strother, Surridge, Wauch.

PLATE 67.

1. Abot, Beale, Bedingfield, Christian, Christopher, Collier, Conradus, Conyngham, Cumberdedge, Cumberlege, Cunningham, Cunninghame, Curwen, Daniel, Daniell, Dicome, Dobbs, Erington, Errington, Freeling, Fribourg, Fylloll, Goodacre, Head, Jemmet, Innes-Ker, Ker, Kokington, Layer, Leigh, Leigh-Hanbury, Lower, Lyell, M'Brair, M'Braire, Manaton, Mathie, Meetekerke, Michelgrove, Morleigh, Neil, Newport, Nicholson, Oliphant, Parish, Perkinson, Ramadge, Ramsey, Savage, Skidmore, Smyth, Stapleton, Swanley, Vignoles, Villages, Wilkinson, Wright, Wynn.
2. Agmondisham, Agmundesham, Anderson, Balberney, Blair, Brocket, Brun, Buck, Cocks, Coggeshall, Crickman, De Hollyngworthe, Denholm, Downes, Fordyce-Dingwall, Fordyce, Galland, Gordon, Græme, Graham, Gullan, Hollingworth, Hopson, Karbyll, Macartney, M'Min, M'Minn, M'Myne, Medford, Park, Perkin, Robarts, Scot, Scott, Simmer, Skae, Symmer, Towers, Van, Webb, Wroughton.
3. Akelond, Ashoe, Atherton, Athorpe, Atterton, Baxter, Beilby, Bell, Bielby; Blagrave, Bolton, Boscawen, Boscowen, Bowes, Bradney, Cay, Chambers, Clements, Colepeper, Cooper, Costello, Cotton, Culpeper, Dillon, Drummond, Du Bois, Enery, Faukenner, Fawkes, Featherstonhaugh, Frank, Franks, Graham, Grandorge, Grain, Gulline, Hadly, Hawk, Hawke, Hawkins, Hay, Hewitson, Hewitt, Hide, Hill, Howson, Incledon, Justice, Kay, Kaye, Kemp, Knox, Lacon, Lacy, Lee, MacEniery, M'Eniery, M'Morran, Morland, Morrice, Nangle, Nicoll, Nolan, Oliphant, O'Nolan, Perkinson, Plaiters, Platers, Porteous, Ralston, Ridgeway, Rose, Rudall, Rudhall, Rythe, Sparhawk, Sparrow, Stratton, Watt, Webber, Williams, Yarworth.
4. Allan, Allen, Anelche, Antisell, Antwisel, Balfour, Blair, Borthwick, Bouvier, Busteed, Chalmers, Coton, Cumming, Dacre, Dorannan, Dugmore, Farquhar, Forbes, Fountain, Jackson, Kinloch, Kinlock, Knox, Macfarlane, M'Nish, M'Vicar, Mansell, Maxwell, Melvine, Monro, Monrose, Montgomery, Morres, Munro, Newbigging, Niblett, Norwood, O'Donavan, O'Dovanan, Pole, Reid, St. Aubyn, Saumarez, Schank, Shank, Smail, Smallpiece, Smith, Treminell, Tremynell, Trivett, Widworthy.
5. Adams, Addagh, Baker, Baunceford, Bayley, Bentley, Bentham, Billingham, Blenkinsopp, Blodlow, Bois, Bokenham, Bonell, Booth, Bowen-Webb, Boyce, Boyse, Brampton, Brent, Brompton, Brooke, Brown, Browne, Bruce, Buckingham, Burgess, Casmajor, Chardin, Clapham, Cliff, Colyear, Coverdale, Coverdall, Crawfield, Crossfield, Cumming, Dansey, Davies, Davis, De Silva, Donelan, Dowson, Drummond, Dupree, Edridge, Edwards, Egerton, Fairfax, Farquhar, Fitz-Water, Ford, Gargate, Gererd, Germin, Germyn, Gibbines, Gore, Gouring, Grace, Græme, Graham, Griffith, Gronow, Gwyn, Hagart, Haggerston, Hatcliff, Holker, Holmes, Hosken, Jarveis, Jarvis, Jefferis, Jones, Kenan, Lamb, Lambert, Lea, Leaton, Lewis, Lincolne, Lloyd, Lows, Ludlow, Lutwidge, M'Diarmid, MacDiarmott, M'Millan, M'Neil, Marney, Mathisson, Mauncell, Meeke, Mills; Modern College, Blackheath; Morgan, Morris, Mostyn, Nanney, Newman, Newton, Norfolk, Northfolke, Ogilvie, Owen, Paget, Parker, Paslew, Patte, Paynell, Peart, Peel, Pellat, Peryan, Price, Raines, Raley, Redington, Richards, Ritson, Rose, Saltren, Seaton, Shaw, Shipton, Simpson, Sloan, Sommers, Sowerby, Stanbury, Stanger, Starr, Stephens, Stevens, Tappin, Thompson, Thorne, Tottenham, Toures, Vaughan, Vernon, Vowe, Westenra, Weyland, Whale, Williams, Wilshere, Wolley, Young.
6. Bell, Boyd, Garvie, Kassye, Miller, Tough.
7. Brews, Brewes, Chesham, Cokfeld, Crew, Crewe, De Brewes, De Kokefield, Sands, Savage, Scudamore.
8. Amand, Amane, Amarme, Don, Hedges, Poynings, Virtue.
9. Abram; African Company of Scotland; Auld, Barclay, Blackwood, Blundestone, Blunstone, Bright, Bruce, Dallyson, Eastchurch, Eiston, Farquharson, Gilchrist, Græme, Hewat, Hewatt, Israel, Jackson, Jaffrey, Jeffrey, Ker, Leson, Lesone, Lysons, Merrifield, Oakey, Pearson, Pinckeney, Purves, Purvis, Saville, Tait, Triggs, Walker.
10. Agar, Allen, Ayloffe, Baett, Batt, Barnes, Baron, Baskett, Basket, Beamish-Bernard, Bell, Bernall, Betton, Birnie, Bischoff, Black, Blaw, Blouyle, Bonell, Bosanquet, Bosworth, Braid, Breck, Breek, Bridges, Bulimore, Cade, Capell, Capon, Charlton, Clarke, Clifden, Cobham, Cookson, Coplestone, Coppenger, Coppinger, Corrie, Corry, Cosins, Cosyns, Coulthand, Cromer, Cruice, Cruise, Cunnington, Currie, Curry, Dalingrugge, Davies, Dennis, Dicey, Dickenson, Diconson, Dillon, Diss, Dixon, Dodwell, Dolton, Dovor, Drane, Drummond, Duncombe, Emes, Emme, English, Esharton, Evens, Ewan, Farquharson, Fife, Fiffe,

PLATE 67—*continued.*

Fitz-John, Ford, Fury, Fyfe, Fyffe, Gaine, Gerandot, Geridot, Glasse, Gold, Goldesburgh, Goold, Grace, Grady, Grant, Griffiths, Grindal, Grindall, Hacklet, Halsbury, Hare, Harrison, Herin, Heron, Hindmarsh, Hoberd, Hobert, Hopkins, Hunter, Husdell, Hutchinson, Hyatt, Ingles, Inglis, Jesse, John, Jones, Joy, Kedmarston, Keith, Kirkman, Kyffyn, Lacy, Langrishe, Layton, Leigh, Levi, Lewins, Llewellyn, Lloyd, Logan, Lomelyng, Loyd, Lynn, M'Candlish, Macduff, Macfie, M'Kenzie, M'Phie, Maddison, Madocks, March, Martyre, Matchett, Matthews, Menet, Menett, Moncrieff, Moncrieffe, Montaguta, Mores, Morres, Moubbray, Mowatt, Mubray, Newlands, Nichol, Nicholson, Nickelson, Nicol, Nicolson, Noland, Nowland, Norman-Lee, Northwood, Ogilvie, Ogilvy, Osborne, Owen, Peace, Pearmain, Pears, Pepper, Percivall, Picken, Picton, Pickton, Pigg, Pomeroy, Pope, Powell, Praed, Priddle, Priestley, Primerose, Prouse, Ravensholme, Read, Repley, Riddell, Ridout, Rishton, Robartes, Rock, Rogerson, Roughsedge, Rowlatt, Rumbold, Russell, Rust, Scot, Scott, Sebright, Selwyn, Seys, Shaw, Shields, Simpson, Spence, Stainsbury, Steuart, Stevens, Stevenson, Stewart, Stockes, Stone, Strange, Strode, Stroode, Stroud, Stroude, Stuart, Taswell, Tatlock, Thomas, Thoroughgood, Throwgood, Tibbet, Titford, Traby, Tyers, Vampage, Van Streyan, Vaughan, Weldon, Wells, Wilcocks, Wilson, Wintringham, Wisham, Wood, Wyse, Yates.

11. Adyer, Aulde, Auld, Courtney, Scot, Walker.
12. Dell, Gipps, Riches, Robertson, Robinson, Tapper, Williamson.
13. Ackworth, Annand, Benyon, Bold, Chisenal, Chisenhall, Clifford, Colley, Cooke, Cooling, Cross, Culling, Davies, De Morton, Duffin, Finch, Foley, Gamage, Grimshaw, Knolles, Lewis, Lovett, Martyn, Morgan, Morton, Parkhurst, Pleasaunce, Reed, Sandes, Sands, Sandy, Sandys, Stern, Woodhouse, Worster.
14. Acheson, Aird, Airth, Aitcheson, Aitchison, Aitkenson, Aitkinson, Akenhead, Alcock, Alexander, Alicock, Allcock, Allen, Allicock, Allicocke, Ard, Atchison, Barloss, Belmore, Beltoft, Beltofts, Blackeston, Blackiston, Blackstone, Blackston, Blakiston, Blakston, Bland, Blaykeston, Bolles, Bolls, Brown, Burgon, Clutton, Coats, Coburn, Cock, Cockburn, Cockburne, Cockridge, Cocks, Cockworthy, Cookworthy, Corrie, Corry, Cotes, Coxon, Coxson, Crow, Currie, Curry, Cush, Cushe, De la Fosse, Delaite, De Lyle, Dewar, Dounie, Downie, Downfield, Ducarel, Eldecur, Elercur, Ellercur, Emmerson, Erington, Errington, Erthe, Forbes, Gael, Gallimore, Grant, Grave, Grubbam, Grubham, Guion, Guyon, Hancock, Handcock, Hellier, Helyard, Hildyard, Hilliard, Hillyard, Holden, Houston-Blakiston, Hyldeard, Ingram, Innes, Irvine, Kellawaye, King, Kognose, Laing, Landle, Langley, Law, Laws, Lee, Le Vavasour, Lodwich, Lodwick, Mackworth, M'Worth, Mathew, Mathieson, Mathison, Milroy, Nowlan, Nowland, Ormistone, O'Slatterie, Perrin, Rig, Rigg, Rochford, Simond, Sinclair, Slater, Slatterie, Standish, Standish-Carr, Stephens, Tamworth, Thorpe, Thring, Tunstall, Turstall, Vavasour, Vawdrey, Williams, Wykes.
15. Bray, Dowland, Gibbe, Gibbs, More.

PLATE 68.

1. Campbell, Champion, Coe, Cother, Laurie, Meakin, Mermyon, Smith.
2. Almard, Armony, Audry, Billing, Billinge, Boddam, Bolland, Bowen, Brice, Burrowes, Burrows, Cavendish, Clonmel, Creake, Denovan, Devereaux, Devereux, Duvernet, Duvernette, Erisey, Forster, Foster, Fothergill, Frothingham, Gadsby, Gage, Glanvile, Glanville, Green, Greene, Grove, Grundin, Hart, Hindman, Hutchison, Jennings, Jones, Lally, Lewin, Lewing, Lewis, Lisle, Lloyd, MacKindlay, Manard, Marnell, Masterson, Mathias, Maynard, Michelson, Montague, Moore, Morris, Nicholson, Noel, Novell, Nowell, Parker, Parkhouse, Parkhurst, Patrick, Pepper, Plant, Polden, Pollard, Puelesdon, Pulesdon, Puleston, Pulleston, Raleigh, Roberts, Robertson, Robinson, Rodie, Rodway, Rogers, Rose, Rosse, Scott-Douglas, Scot, Scott, Scote, Scriven, Sisson, Steade, Steede, Thomas, Thorold, Townsend, Trevanion, Trollop, Troup, Walkington, Wear, Weare, Wordesworth, Wrench, Wynne, Yarrow.
3. Angolisme, Austin.
4. Bestroe, Jeffreys, Pratt, Dawbeney, Doleman, Forican, Huskisson, Ledgcomb, Lynes, Maddocks, Oliphant, Risdon, Sanders, Saunders, Sutton, Throckmorton, Throgmorton.
5. Harvey.
6. Bertram, Bettes, Blunt, Bockland, Borland, Galton, Hastings, Hollingshed, Massy, Radcliff, Ratcliffe, Walcot, Walcott, Wharton, Whitbroke.
7. Behethland, Brichen, Durban, Durbin.
8.
9. Cossar, Cosser, Ferguson, Fergusson, Gardner, Innes, M'Innes.
10. Badelismere, Badelsmere, De Segrave, Flint, Kennerley.
11. Bowyer, Bylney, Connell, Halpin, Higginson, Kerdiston, Lauder, Lawder, Law, Laxton, Luckin, Tassie, Whorwood.
12 Absalem, Absalom, Absolom, Absolum, Absolon, Ascum, Bernheim, Blizard, Boutfleur, Cairnes, Chastelin, Cheslin, Clarke, Cope, Cowie, Dealtry, Deyvil,

PLATE 68—*continued.*

Doketone, Docton, French, Gay, Goulton, Grant, Greethead, Hay, Howson, Hill, Hinson, Lyndwood, Macaul, Montogomery, Mountford, Mountfort, Newdegate, Newdigate, Newport, Norbury, Toler, Oketon, Okton, Pancefoote, Pickering, Plantagenet, Pottman, Reede, Richards, Richars, Rogers, Rolland, Schoffield, Schofield, Sherbrooke, Smith, Sparkes, Stoddyr, Taddy, Udney, Udnie, Warden, Wardor, Willcocks.

13. Boileau, Bulley, Clavel, Clavell, Tourner, Turner.
14. Abbs, Abraham, Blackwood, Blunt, Coke, Cooke, Drayton, Fairbairn, Fairweather, Farquharson, Florio, Fonnereau, Forbes, Freebairn, Grevis, Hay, Hewson, Jack, Janssen, Joanes, Jones, Ker, Kerr, M'Cleod, M'Hardie, Mackenzie, M'Kenzie, Macleod, M'Leod; Marischal College, Aberdeen; Mason, Masson, Mellis, Moffat, Nairne, Oliphant, Pass, Pearson, Pegge, Pitcairn, Pratt, Reilly, Richmond, Rodwell, Routh, Rowdon, Rutt, Sotheby.
15. Jossey, Townsend.

PLATE 69.

1. Parkinson.
2. Parker.
3. Parr.
4. Parsons.
5. Peacock.
6. Hitchens, Hitchins, Partridge, Patrich.
7. Reeve.
8. Pedyward.
9. Reid.
10. Reynes.
11. Reppes, Repps.
12. Rhan, Wrench.
13. Rhodes.
14. Rich.
15. Reynolds.

PLATE 70.

1. Carpenter, Conesby, Coningesby, Capel-Coningsby, Coningsby, Conisbie, Coney, Cony, Leverton, Purslow, Warrender.
2. Appelton, Appolton, Hart, Ridgeway, Ridgway.
3. Connel, Connell, Ringewood, Ringwood.
4. Copinger, Cruttendon, Ord, Orde.
5. Arblester, Arablester, Areblaster, Berring, Coleman, Fox, Foxall, Holway, Hallington, Hallowtown, Hodges, Holway, Kyngesley, Purkis, Wooton, Wootton.
6. Coote, Cricket, Crickitt.
7. Couston, Drummond, Leving, Levinge, Lord, Tatton.
8. Cockfield, Hayne, Haynes, Steer, Studley.
9. Cove, Guthry, Heber, Middleton, Pengelley, Scales.
10. Coucher, Cowcher, Hodiswell, Welles.
11. Borely, Borseley, Cornwall, Donand, Seaton, Seton.
12. Collison, Forest, Harling, Harlingham, Holliday, Leeds, Marney, Tuberwille.
13. Ackelom, Bendlowes, Cromie, Cruell, Crull, De Kyme, Fitz-Maurice, Lambart, Lambert, Petty, Petty-Fitzmaurice.
14. Corrie, Corry, Hanckford, Hendrie, Hendry, Hyman, Soper, Sutton.
15. Bailey, Bringham, Crump, Crumpe, Gordon, Macbean, M'Intosh, MacIntosh. Sutherland.

PLATE 71.

1. Anderley, Crafton, Malton, Seagar, Seager, Spear, Symonds.
2. Amsdem, Amsdon.
3. Anderson, Anderton, Bowley, Fitz-Allen, Judge, Pickering, Wordie.
4. Bellet, Cleeve, Fox, Franklin, Gysors, Longsdon, Lyford, M'Pherson, Papeworth, Purser, Reason, Reson, Reynold, Rushe, Williams.
5. Beckering, Bekering, Fielding, Gedney.
6. Amborow, Anbury, Anborow, Barker, Beaumont, Benson, Bere, Brereton, Brewster, Chamberlain, Fitz-Harry, Forth, Freckelton, Freckleton, Fulford, Gimber, Langham, Langholme, Longham, Milburn, Spence, Travis.
7. Chapman, Colles, Colvil, Colville, Ingle, Lander, Todd.
8. Catznellage, Chauster, Elphinstone, Wayer.
9. Chapman, Chisholm, Dumbreck, Etton, Gwyn, Leslie, Lyon, O'Neylan.
10. Drysdale.
11. Benjamin, Cuckborne, Dundas, Heaill, Mansel, Mansell, Maunseil, Swift.
12. Drummond.
13. Aldred, Bonnett, Dunkin, MacDonald, Macdonald. M'Donald, MacDonnell, Patch, Storr, Wentworth,
14. Eves, Geyton, Mann.
15. Crookshank, Dunbar, Eynford, Eynsworth, Hellis, Howe, Howse.

PLATE 72.

1. Bagnell.
2. Athanray, Bagot, Dayrell, Delaval, Dyer-Swinnerton, Gardiner, Garforth, Gason, Ives, Jones, Sedley, Sideley, Sidley,

PLATE 72—*continued.*

Smith, Smyth, Swynerton, Wetnall, Whitington, Yate, Yates.
3. Baddiford.
4. Caldwell, Jodrell, Parker.
5. Baldwin, Cadye, Kadye.
6. Darnell.
7. Edmonds.
8. Caird, Caldmore.
9. Bulwer, Edolphe, Fowke, Rugge.
10. Edwards.
11. Dalrymple.
12. Almond, Crompe, Falch.
13. Fardell.
14. Dankyrsley.
15. Baker, Gard.

PLATE 73.

1. Abbett, Abett, Alate, Allatt, Allett, Christian, Clarke, Goodrood, Hyde, Ipres, Keyte, Kite, Leigh, Priese, Spilsburie.
2. Abbey, Beaver, Blackie, Culmer, Gore, Linch, Main, Maskell, Moyse, Villeboies.
3. Abelhall, Ablehall, Binks, Darnall, Darnel, Darnol, Horseford, Meoles.
4. Babbwell, Babwell, Brew, Foston, Harold, Harrold, Onmany, Skipwith, Turvile, Wingate, Wyngate, Yates.
5. Bacheler, Bacholor, Bachelour, Batchellor, Batchelor, Rain, Raine.
6. Baggs, Hepburn, Lynan, Valange, Wallange.
7. Billcliffe, Blondell, Brand, Colet, Drake, Drumson, Ecles, Forbes, Garrard-Drake, Gessors, Jeynes, Lapp, Law, Madyston, Meschines, Milburne, Pomfrett, Pritchard, Rivett, Stane, Waddington, Willey, Willy, Wright.
8. Burke, Ogilvie, Ogilvy.
9. Borston, Cairncross, Dalzell, Durnford, M'Guire, Macjure, Macquire, M'Quire, Pring, Thetford, Wimbolt.
10. Astrovel, Dacres, Lesly, Pelham, Peters, Provost, Wakehurst.
11. Bucton, Bunbury, Domvile, Domville, Graham.
12. Bradwell, Carnie, Corningham, Deline, Grant, Haig, Hamilton-Dalrymple, Hornsey, Kylle, Le Roache, Langlois, Mackenzie, M'Kenzie, NacNeil, M'Neil, Macneill, Mather, Ouchterlony, Pittman, Reoch, Roche, Rowche, Sandeman, Scarsborough, Southall, Walker.
13. Boradaile, Borradaile, Borrodaile, Colfox.
14. Booker, Eastman, Loges, Saul, Saule.
15. Bell, Boon, Boone, Cairns, Desbrisay, Dynham, Eckingham, Fitz-Piers, Levinge, Stasam.

PLATE 74.

1. Ellison.
2. Ellis.
3. Elphingston.
4. Elmsall-Greaves.
5. Elmes, Ewarby, Gregory, Thornton.
6. Elwill.
7. Farwell.
8. Farquhar-Gray.
9. Feldingham, Fillingham.
10. Shute.
11. Farmer.
12. Ferguson.
13. Gardin, Graden, Greiden.
14. Fell.
15. Gardner, Moret.

PLATE 75.

1. Hardyman.
2. Hamilton.
3. Johnson, Ritchie.
4. Copland, Gysseling, Irvine.
5. Diskens, Goodenough, Harbord.
6. Enswell, Entwissell, Janson, Lloyd.
7. Irvine, Lile, Lille.
8. Cheverell, Cheverill, Fitz-Maurice, Grossett, Halcro, Innes, Morehead, Penrey.
9. Jackson.
10. Jandrill.
11. Hardieman, Hardyman, Jebb, Lant, Spiller, Trist.
12. Jenkens.
13. Cumming, Jenner.
14. Hansfell.
15. Jervoise-Clarke.

PLATE 76.

1. Acland, Palmer, Philips.
2. Jarveis, Jervis-Rickets.
3. Agad, Trotter.
4. Acton.
5. Abtot, Cottesford.
6. Aito, Auito.
7. Baber, Cramer.
8. Dering, Upton.
9. Ash, Babthorp, Fanshawe, Olive.
10. Caddon.
11. Badder, Madder, Modder, Stocket.
12. Cadiman, Douthwaite, Nesham.
13. Dade, Scambler, Veale, Vele.
14. Cabourne, Cabne.
15. Daniell, Leishman.

PLATE 77.

1. Burt, Burtt, Mellor, Neave.
2. Brander, Brandon, Burye, Durie, Dury, Hodges, Knife, Skey, Smyth, Wegget, Wiggett.
3. Butcher, Creping, Crepping, Fleury, Mackay, Martin, Martine, Mulbery, Mulbury.
4. Abinger, Comberton, Cotter, Liddle, Nefield, Nesfield, Scarlet, Skarlett.
5. Brand, Callis, Lightbourne. Lucas, Thornton.
6. Bumstead, Bumsted, Charrington, Corke, Knyvett.
7. Bourden, Old, Strang, Strong.
8. Boyes, Boys.
9. Brenchesley, Brenchley.
10. Bourke.
11. Barrat, Barratt, Crichton, Daniel, Mill, Milne, Tighe.
12. Currey, Currie, Deschamps, Fowkes, Narboon, Narboone, Prowse.
13. Smyth.
14. Borlase, Croachrod, Fleetwood.
15. Brett, Dalbie, Dalby.

PLATE 78.

1. Chastelon, Farr, Favell. Glendenning, Glendonwyn, Glendowing, Haviland, Sterling, Tate.
2. Durant.
3. Ryan.
4. Amarle, Armarle.
5. Frost.
6. Foote, Greer, Rowe.
7. Forbes.
8. Carrol, Carroll, Francois, Franks, Hewett, Hewitt, Kerslake, O'Carroll, Welcome, Whitmore, Witmore.
9. Bloodworth, Forrest, Izon, Letton, M'Daniel, McGougan, Thomson, Rowell, Wylidon.
10. Jefferyes.
11. Abbot, Algoe.
12. Dunn, Dunne, Foleborne, Irvine, Smythe.
13. Chaucer, Fletwick, Graydon.
14. Bourcher, Bourchir, Bourchier, Flight, Wrey.
15. Boddie, Boddy, Dymoke, Dymock, Varley, Wagstaff, Whithers.

PLATE 79.

1. Hope, Scott-Hope.
2. Aubin, Graham-Maxwell, Hardacre, Hoseason.
3. Bassinges, Hill, Mayhew, Roos, Ross, Zachert, Zachet.
4. Hillary.
5. Aikman, Clesby, Danford, Hind, Sinclair.
6. Ferris, Kellock, Mayo.
7. Aighton, Alexander.
8. Hoadley.
9. Cox, Farley, Power, Squire.
10. Garling, Robsert.
11. Hockin, Spencer.
12. Goldie, Hansard, Harringworth, Kibble, Latimer, Lionnel, Rufus, Rutledge.
13. Genn, Rotham, Sprencheaux, Springhose, Thomas.
14. Dunbar, Fullwood, Lowry, McArther, M'Arthur, Maudit, Sibbald.
15. Gidion, Harden, Hardin, Longman.

PLATE 80.

1. Foleborne, Gilpin, Grierson, Sterry.
2. M'Hattie.
3. Birte, Grover.
4. Bodenham, Dyne, Dynne, Kynaston.
5. De Mowbray, Fitz-Geoffry, Gandy, Gandey, Goldman, Gracie, Hoar, Houton, Lavell, Lawrie, Lepard, M'Cloud, Mowbray, Pendret, Penrith, Pondrell, Reynell, St. Clere, Stranger.
6. Chamberlaine, Chamberlayne, Mainwaring, Manwairing, St. Amond, Wooldridge.
7. Arnald, Arnauld, Bourk, Charteris, Charters, Chartres, Gillespie, Keat, M'Intosh, Macintosh, M'Kean, Mumford, Shives, Tiller, Winterbotham, Withypoule.
8. Fitton, Fitz-Hugh, Steers.
9. Bower, Bowman, Coults, Fiton.
10. Huntercomb.
11. Gunton, Mordant, Mordaunt, Shipley.
12. Harries, Huckmore.
13. Chetwode, Haldimand, Holl, Houell, Ramsey, Sherman, Tufton.
14. Groine, Groom, Groome.
15. Howard.

PLATE 81.

1. Carpenter, Goodlad; Merchant Company, Leith; Merchant Company, Edinburgh; Nairn, Nairne, Reynolds, St. Lize, Staley, Stayley.
2. Elerkar, Fitz-Richard, Durham, Kergourdenac, Naufan, Nanphan, Vickery.
3. Chetwyn, Collins, Lightfoot, Logan.
4. Adyn, Anmers, Anners, Argal, Argall, Argell, Argill, Arkybus, Ashton, Atherley, Atkinson, Auld, Bamford, Baumford, Baunford, Bates, Bawtre, Bawtree, Beal, Bilesby, Birney, Bow, Branfell, Brusell, Buchan, Buckle, Burdett, Burghill, Burnett, Burney, Burnie, Carr, Carr-Standish, Carter, Chaigneau, Chalmers, Chambers, Cheese, Chiefly, Cinsallagh, Crokey, Crynes, Dalrymple, David, Davis, Denham, Dodswall, Dodswell, Dowell, Edge-

PLATE 81—*continued.*

worth, Edridge, Edwards, Ennew, Flower, Flowre, Foote, Ford, Galbraith, Garnier, Gordon, Grubb, Gunner, Harper, Harridge, Haskins, Hawden, Hawtre, Hende, Hinde, Holmes, Home, Hose, Hoskyns, Houison, Hume, Jefferyes, Jefferys, Jones, Joulden, Kirkham, Kettleby, Kittelby, Kittleby, Knot, Knott, Leighton, Lighton, Long, Lorimer, Lowndes, Lynn, Lyon, Macgregor, M'Gregor, Mackey, MacKnight, M'Knight, M'Leod, MacMurdoch, M'Naught, M'Nicoll, M'Quaid, M'Taggart, Maitland, Markland, Marsham, Massey, Maud, Maude, Melders, Meredith, Meredith-Warter, Merling, Morson, Mortlock, Munn, Murdoch, Nearns, Nicholson, Nicolson, Ogilvie, Ogilvy, Payne, Pearsall, Pearse, Peckover, Pentland, Perks, Perrot, Pickernell, Pickford, Pigou, Plasto, Portal, Potts, Pratte, Price, Pulteney, Rackham, Rawlins, Renwick, Rolfe, Ross, Rowland, Rowsewell, Ryle, Scot, Scott, Scotland, Shelbery, Shelbury, Silvester, Sim, Sime, Simm, Smyth, Stanford, Stebbing, Steele, Steell, Steuart, Stewart, Sumner, Surman, Tawse, Toole, Trimwell, Tuson, Tweddale, Unett, Vylgus, Waddell, Wakeman, Walters, Wartnaby, Weddell, Weatherston, Wetherton, Wheterton, Whitchurch, White, Whitington, Whitwell, Wigston, Williams, Wilson, Wolin, Worge, Wrey, Yeates, Yeats, Yerbine.

5. Allman, Alman, Eyre, Eyre-Radcliffe-Livingstone, Helias, M'Cull, Pack, Packe, Westbrook, Younger.
6. Basset, Bassett, Berryman, Bodelsgate, Clarke, Coleman, Curwan, Deacon, Dethick, Dunbar, Earl, Essington, Fletcher, Goorick, Guilamore, Heaton, Heigham, Hewgell, Hewgill, Ibbetson, Jones, Kean, Leigh, Lloyd, Mannell, Meynell, O'Grady, Partridge, Prideaulx, Rotland, Roushland, Rushe, Rutland, Slade, Slader, Smyth, Steed, Verst, Warner, Whippy, Yate.
7. Andrews, Bagshole, Bagshote, Barton, Blackshame, Dupa, Duppa, Graham, Gruben, Lawrence, O'Reilly, Querleton, Querlton, Tolley, Trelawney, Wight.
8. Agmondsham, Annabell, Annable, Annables, Barham, Board, Brees, Breeze, Busk, Clelland, Cochrane, Cochran, Coppendale, Forster, Gordon, Halliburton, Halyburton, Leith, M'Corquodell, M'Corquodill, Meales, Nethersole, Noel, Parry, Passmore, Rae, Slade, Strachan, Stradling, Writington.
9. Bosworth, Coane, Dundee, Gray, Rait, Torre, Watson.
10. Aysingcourt, Aysyngcourt, Berey, Craford, Deacons, Deedes, Games, Godard, Harty, Kniveton, Knyfton, Leids, Merlyon, Sadler, Shiel, Stein, Stephens, Theshmaker, Wilmer.
11. Abel, Aldborough, Amond, Arcedeckne, Archdeckne, Athil, Athill, Athol, Athyll, Basnett, Bell, Birrel, Birrell, Black, Bloor, Bloore, Buck, Bucke, Busbridge, Clarkson, Colby, Coley, Cree, Crewker, Cripps, Crips, Curtis, Davis, Donald, Druce, Graham, Greg, Greig, Greive, Hagges, Hardie, Henry, Holdich, Holdiche, Hone, Jardelay, Kirke, Laurenson, Lauriston, Leatham, Macarmick, M'Coul, M'Cubbin, MacDougall, M'Dougall, M'Gregor, M'Hardie, M'Kellar, M'Kellor, Majendie, Millward, Molony, Oakeley, Partheriche, Partherické, Pilgrim, Plott, Rice, St. Amond, Saunderson, Strangforth, Stratford, Tregose, Trent, Tufnal, Tuftnell, Wingate.
12. St. John.
13. Norris, Parr, Vernon.
14. Brade, Browne, Calderwood, Crisie, Gausen, Gaussen, Honeywill, Kerry, M'Crire, Petty, Petty-Fitzmaurice, Shillinglaw, Suttie, Templer.
15. Abilem, Adair, Bond, Brackenbury, Buller, Dunston, Duston, Gaudine, Gawsworth, Haly, Heselrige, Irton, Lansford, M'Nab, M'Nabb, Magill, Molynes, Molyns, Monington, Morgan, Mounsher, Muir, Newbery, Pecksall, Prendergast, Renwick, Rochead, Selby, Stapleton, Stewart, Tremenheere, Urby, Wendesley.

PLATE 82.

1. Aphery.
2. Allardice, Allerdice, Allieson, Allison, Burland, Gedding, Geding, Lynam, Merton, Powle.
3. Aundeligh, Bawdewyn, Bawdwen, Drought, Handley, Hanley, Lumb.
4. Alanson, Allanson, Allaunson, Allenson.
5. Argum, Argun, Argune, Briwer, Briwere, Molloy, Park, Poulden, Reade, Reid.
6. Alley, Forty, Hawle, Marner, Stillington.
7. Brockholes, Coghlan, Coghlen, Cowan, De Harcla, Harcle, Lacy, Neale, Nele, Vaire.
8. Brandt, Maxwell.
9. Apreece, Brodrick, Rice.
10. Ballenger, Beauvoir, Brickenden, Bury, Castleton, D'Oyley, Drax, Fitz-Osbert, Forman, Knyuet, Knyvett, Man, Mann, Maun, Owen, Raven.
11. Brattle, Mackleans.
12. Browne.
13. Broadstone.
14. Creting, Debnam, Farrel, Farrell, Mildred.
15. Broheir, Brohier, Haines, Hutton, Warden.

PLATE 83.

1. Beauchampe, Bruget, Crost, Fagan, Greville, Hutchinson, Scales, Swann, Sybyle, Vipont, Vipount.
2. Brudenell.
3. Almayne, Burard, Sackvil, Sackvile, Sackwille.
4. Bewcham, Beweham, Burnet, Burnett, Faquier, Virtue.
5. Burg, Lant, Sprye.
6. Burslam, Burslem, Comberford, Mayce, Nonwers, Norwers, Nowers, Straiton.
7. Codd, Codde, Dunkley, Foxley, Godwin, Jausselin, Jocelyn, Jocelyne, Kendrick, Paumier.
8. Brook, Brooke.
9. Coombes, Coombs, Horan, Locke, Lunden, Lundin, Purchas.
10. Doran.
11. Briscoe, Briscowe, Monckton, Mongdene, Mongtown, Monkton, Paul.
12. Dring, Kennaway, Leeson, Templeman, Viney.
13. Ackland, Acland, Akeland, Akland, Cleland, Cleiland, Cleilland, Cleland, Jenny, Jobson.
14. Dickenson, Hay.
15. Denman, Dunstavile, Dunstaville, Garret, Hewetson, Sturton.

PLATE 84.

1. Cockerell.
2. Yvain.
3. Dove, Felbridge, Nicholas, Nicholl, Schneider, Sherfield.
4. Riley.
5. Rogers.
6. Sedgewick, Somner.
7. Ogilvy, Plomer.
8. Fermoy, Roche.
9. Gilbert, Macklin, M'Lin, Pranell, Prannell, Tripp.
10. Porte.
11. Pringle.
12. Pomeroy.
13. Bernil, Birnal, Birnall, Clayley, Colthurst, Curtis, Dickenson, English, Go[illegible]lin, Joanes, Leigh, Lewis, Mathews, Morier, Nicholson, Pepper, Plunkett, Read, Rumbold, Rutter, Thomas, Wortling.
14. Roberts.
15. Phillip.

PLATE 85.

1. Deton, Harlewen, Jonas, Lindsay, Pontifex, Pott, Prother, Vale.
2. Bradshagh, Bradshaigh, Bradshaw, Collingwood, Kneller.
3. Amcotts, Ayncotts, Bloundell, Dighton.
4. Ingeham, Ingham, Kitchen, Salman, Salmon.
5. Blower.
6. Affleck, Crofton, Dunford, Johnson, Longchamp, Longchampe, Loughnan, Mitchael, Mitchell, Scot, Swinton, Yuille, Yule.
7. Blamore, Britweesil, Corbally, Coupland, Crab, Dudman, Guthrie, Hebert, Hoddy, Hody, M'Can, Maclaughlan, M[illegible]an, Moult, Penrose, Redingham, Sal[illegible]nd, Willeigh, Willeley.
8. Capes.
9. Ormsby, Spottiswood.
10. Blizard, Blizzard, Boyer, Dymond, O[illegible]vie
11. Le Blanc.
12. Eeles, Harrison, Latouche, La Touche.
13. Albyn.
14. Hamond, Heegnie, Hinde-Hodgson, Kenyon, Malton.
15. Brydall, Hiatt, Payne.

PLATE 86.

1. Cooper, Cowper, Creeck, Gilmore, Græme, Heriot, Krag, Kragg, M'Kenzie, Mitchell, Pearson, Ross, Skeen, Stevenson, Wodderspoon.
2. Beaver, Blake, Cann, Catesby, Coventry, Derhaugh, Freeland, Harvey, Hervey, Hervy, Partridge, Pettet, Pettit, Puddesey, Pudsey, Pusey, Rosseter, Shrimpton, Taylour.
3. Broad, Dox, Doxey, Govett, MacConach, MacConachie, Macfarlane, M'Farlane, M'Farlin.
4. Aberbuthnot, Arbuthnot, Dinevyn, Dirwyn, Fynes, Hewes, Holbicke, Merrill, Pitson, Purdie, Purdy, Smyth, Sowerby, Tomlin, Troyhin, Vigures,
5. Dobie, Gilmer, Gilmour, Isely, Isley, Lutwidge, MacMaure, Sayers.
6. Compton, Cussans, Jackson, Le Hunt, Lockhart.
7. Cely, Ceely, Deraw, Hambleton, Wilford.
8. Almiger, Armeier, Armiger, Bowyer, Cosen, Cotell, Cottell, Cuthell, Cuthill, Cutler, Gooche, Good, Hamill, Hovell.
9. Aunsham, Awnsam, Bullingham, Bustin, Cenino, Lowdham, Pringle.
10. Crisp, Offley, Roche.
11. Bromeley, Bromley.
12. Callore, Dineley, Estote, Leeson, Ponsonby.
13. Bury, Bushrudd, Irby, Reeve, Reve.
14. Douglas, Fitz-John, Julian, Julion, Macbride, Redley, Stead.
15. Burnel, Burnell, Lyngard, Lyngharde, Phillip, Skepper.

PLATE 87.

1. Aifler, Aigler, Ayler, Filkin, Filkyn, Harvey, Renney, Sargant, Sargeant, Tullock.
2. Agruall, Alley, Alye, Gritton, Singleton.
3. Aermine, Airmine, Armine, Elworth, Frame, Goold, Manchester.
4. Blenerhaset, Blenerhasset, Bleverhasset, Bridgeman, Bridgman, Bridget, Fox, Foxe, Fyler, Brierly, Crosthwaite, Jobber, Kirk, Leslie, Parkin, Todd, Warter, Wartur, Westmoreland, Whytehead.
5. Agnew, Agneu, Baratty, Barron, Hallow, Luce, Malbone, Singleton, Stray, Surman.
6. Broun, Brown, Brownrig, Brownrigg, Coxan, Coxen, Ensor, Fielden, Haugh, Hoppare, Lorimer, Marks, Nyssell, Pugh, Watkins, Whatley, Worsley, Wortley.
7. Aile, Ailes, Armestrang, Armstrang, Armstrong, Ayles, Brace, Bullo, Bulow, Constable, Couper, Roachead.
8. Canham, Ducie, Duffy, Dunies, Kennet, Kennett, Pedder, Walford, Wallford.
9. Canceller, Cancellor.
10. Boswell, Key, Naylor, Prothers, Tomes, Toms.
11. Harrison.
12. Armeston, Armestone, Aske, Aspall, Barton, Beath, Beith, Bieth, Bodenham, Bonham, Borodaile, Bright, Castell, Creed, Croft, Cross, Dennis, De Grey, Draycot, Draycott, Elloway, Grey, Guilford, Hull, Immins, Kighley, Kightley, Littleton, M'Lean, Messye, Meysey, Pemberton, Porter, Rookewood, Stewart, Stovin, Tonkin, Warren, Westropp, Wilkin, Wright.
13. Barnes, Lachlan, Wood.
14. Barwell, Eland, Elland, Elphingston, Hendley, Lodington, Turyn, Woodroffe.
15. Allport, Clunes, Comb, Combe, Cratford, Eldershaw, Faunce, Fleming, Hare, Hunn, Markoe, Marks, Prestwold.

PLATE 88.

1. Philips, Phillips, Poley, Polley, Pooley, Sammes.
2.
3. Awdrey, Awndye, Breton, Bretton, Saint Owen.
4. Bardwell, Cosby, Cottesmore, Woods.
5. Broadbent, Lennie, Sysington.
6. Boak, Crumpton, Festing, Frend, Keenlyside, Kirkhoven, Redmond, Saphar, Scott, Wells.
7. Aitkens, Antrim, Artked, Atwood, Austin, Auston, Bollers, Daniell, Devey, Lucas, MacDonnel, Maundrell, Proven, Rohan.
8. Bewshin.
9. Bowen, Boydell, Fray, Fraye, Hurt, Motton, Randall, Ruff.
10. Atholl, Glenlyon, Maynell, Menell, Meynell, Murray, Murry.
11. Kirby, Kirkby, Mackenzie, M'Kenzie, Thompson.
12. Broadhurst, Fennor, Goband, Legget, Murray.
13. Bunting, Hulbert, Larayne, Lareyn, Skene, Spilman, Staines, Stains, Stevenson, Stevenstone.
14. Markham.
15. Colton, Cusach, Cusack, Cusecke.

PLATE 89.

1. Ahem, Aimgevyne, Brown, Broun, Burnet, Finncane, Garginton, Garwinton, Grumley, Hyett-Adams, Symonds.
2. Adams, Banger, Bladen, Boidell, Carpenter, Cruice, Cruise, De Vallance, Drury, Ford, Fuller, Gale, Hunter, Lefroy, Lloyd, Lynacre, Lynaker, M'Taggart, Mill, Shiffner, Statham.
3. Aigles, Amiel, Ankyrsley, Aygle, Bagshaw, Bellingham, Delaplaunch, De la Plaunch, Done, Duncan, Fennel, Fennell, Forrester, Hall, Holding, Hornby, Hull, Kyd, Kyde, Loudon, Lowthian, Petit, Pourie, Powrie, Purie.
4. Amyand, Barclay, Bolger, Cressenor, Cressner, Duberley, Duberly, Granger, Hand, Kennoway, Kirkton, Kirton.
5. Bamme, Baum, Kingdom, Longhurst, Mackiegan, Tutt.
6. Barke.
7. Arundel, Arundell, Blage, Blake, Cardiffe, Duperon, Eland, Elland, Eyland, Fyske, Heyland, How, Lawson, Mell, Monckton, Overton, Proctor.
8. Beringham, Berringham, Boyd, Clement, Cranford, Delaplaunch, Devonshire, Lunden, Lundin, Miller, Millman, Roddam, Rosselyne, Sibbald, Tinkler, Weldon.
9. Anlet, Anlett, Carey, Faulder, Fulwer, Sherfeild, Wheatley.
10. Alvares, Craig, Dillon, Elstob, Eurn, Ewing, Frew, Gladhill, Henlock, Holburne, Hulburn, Inglis, Lamb, Lambe, Liddell, Lidell, Liddiard, Roberts, Stable, Starr, St. Lyz.
11. Bitterley, Dockenfield, Dokenfield, Duckinfield, Duckingfield, Dukenfield, Falkiner, Karben, Lovelass.
12. Dobbs.
13. Byford, Byfford, Corner, Eagle, Warren.
14. Adam, Adamson, Addie, Adie, Aedie, Andesley, Backie, Constantyne, Dernford, Downie, Fetherston, Kingley, Nadler.
15. Ekins, Neke, Northever, Twinnell.

PLATE 90.

1. Brooke, Gambell, Gamble, Hornby, M'Guarie, Macquarie, Malone.
2. Lanyon.
3. Long-bow-String-Makers, Luke, Reilly, Scopham, Scopyn.
4. Benyngton, Champernon, Cunningham, Henley, Jepine, Morland, Pomeroy, Popingay.
5. Freeston, Freston.
6. Aselock, Blades, Blaydess, Blaydes-Marvel, Bower, Braybrook, Clark, Clifford, Desbrowe, Ellerker, Georges, Griffin, Haigh, Hall, Jeaffreson, Jefferson, Knight, Kyrell, Leslie-Melville, M'Killop, Melveton, Mill, Morham, Patterson, Tanner, Tayloure, Thayer, Wilson.
7. Berwick.
8. Bacche, Bache.
9. Acland, Awdry, Bland-Davidson, Boyle, Boyley, Doran, Fuller.
10. Castleton, Chester, Farington, Farrington, Glover, Ilderton, Loader, Lowther, Monck, Monke, Muncke, Pirton, Reed, Ring, Salvin.
11. Hadwen, De Montmorency.
12. De Clifford, Southwell.
13. Reynolds-Morton, Moreton, Morton.
14. Duff, Lecaufield, Quin, Statham, Windham, Wyndham.
15. Carthew, Coote, Crockat, Crockett, Ducket, Gettens, Kilburne, Kirwan.

PLATE 91.

1. Estoft, Flanagan, Godsaloe, Godschall, Herriot, Herriott, Macpherson, M'Pherson, Martin, Morice, Newsham, Upton.
2. Chick, Chickley, Mair, Moodie, Pyne, Valentine.
3. Delafeld, Delafield, Vachell.
4. Craigg, Fall, Mewbery, Orr, Sideserf, Sidserf, Spedding, Sydserfe, Walker.
5. Chetham, Lutton, Maitland, Travers, Walker.
6. Bowyer, Herworth, Leche, Leitch, Nowell, O'Flynn, Vaughan, Yarworth.
7. Ascough, Ascue, Asken, Askene, Aston, Astonne, Ayscough, Barnardiston, Chamberlain, Chamberlayn, Macklin, Millington, Zouch, Zouche.
8. Aaron, Aarons Aaroons, Aron.
9. Adcock, Addcock, Aston, Babington, Bloomfield, Broke, Burry, Cholwich, Cholwick, Clark, Elderton, Free, Hall, Jollie, Lochore, Lowry, Morris, Richards, Ross, Sutter, Swiney, Tod, Todd, Waller, Whitbread.
10. Begbie, Bellomont, Cairleon, De Bellomont, Faulkner, Irons, Molineaux, Pugh, Rudding, Sagrenor, Stewins, Symington.
11. Argall, Asgile, Badby, Brett, Dempsey, Dernford, Hipkiss, Paris.
12. Airey, Andrea, St. Andrews, Bottiler, Botiler, Cairnes, Cairns, Caus, Crawfurd, Curryer, De Memburgh, Erisey, Farby, Fiddes, Golden, Hamilton, Herries, St. Andrew, Severn, Severne, Spranger, Wifield, Winckworth.
13. Bedford, Bourch, Brown, By, Chalmers, Dummer, Farlough, Hathaway, Hatheway, Hayman, Hayward-Curtis, Leycester, Marke, Markes, Marks, Nolan, Orde, Penny, Phillips, Plumerage, Scobell, Terry.
14. Amos, Barrow, Beckwith, Bell, B[illegible]ingham, Blyth, Bolles, Bondiville, Bonvile, Boteshed, Botockshed, Bowles, Brores, Buck, Broadockshaw, Brodockshaw, Buckley, Buxton, Caddell, Cadell, Campbell, Carr, Cathie, Chapman, Cheyter, Cheytor, Clapcott, Colleton, Collingwood, Colquhon, Colquhoun, Copenger, Crawford, Crowton, Cuerden, Cure[illegible], Dalrymple, Dear, Denny, Dillwyn, D[illegible], Dolling, Done, Duff, Edwards, Elven, Fawcett, Forbes, Forbes-Leith, Foster, Fowles, Fraser, Frend, Fulton, Gaddes, Gaddez, Gallay, Galle, Galley, Geddes, Geddies, Giffard, Gifford, Gilleanks, Gordon, Gould, Grandgeorge, Graungeorge, Grimston, Grimstone, Gunter, Guthries, Harneys, Harnous, Harris, Hart, Heaton, Hendry, Herns, Herries, Hill, Hobkins, Hollingbury, Hunter, Hyde, Keith, Keverdon, Kirkpatrick, Knightley, Knightly, Kyle, Laird, Lampard, Laven, Liberton, Litster, Lloyd, Lovibond Macadam, MacCarthy, M'Adam, Martin, Marton, Maxwell, Margoutz, M[illegible], Meikle, M'Murray, Moldford, Morgan, Mortimer, Murray, Nodin, Nott, Nourse, Noyes, Ogilvie, Ogilvy-John, Paley, Parker, Peat, Perison, P[illegible], Perott, Phelan, Plompton, Plomton, Popham, Power, Poynton, Raper, Roberts, Rockley, Roe, Rokley, Rollo, Rooe, Rotheram, Rowe, Ryvell, Scott, Seaton, Semple, Skene, Snape, Snappe, Snepp, Spence, Spring, Springe, Stamford, Stanley, Stawton, Stepkins, Steventon, Sulliard, Tatenhall, Tredermick, Westall, Whately, Younger, Youngrave.
15. Amorie, Amery, Brampton, Damer, D'Amorie, Nesbitt, Ogilvy, Routh.

PLATE 92.

1. Acford, Affordbie, Affordby, Alexander, Avern, Barstow, Belches, Belshes, Bennie, Benny, Benzie, Binnie, Binny, Blacker, Blaker, Blaney, Bowen, Bruce, Collyngs, Dance, Dannsey, Darley, Dauvergeue, De Cowey, Dunbar, Elmeet, Fry, Gisborne, Hamilton, Hepburn, Lewes, Lewis, Neat, Pritchard, Ramsay, Rutherford, Sarebruche, Smyth, Studholme, Timson, Twentyman, Whinfield, Yates.
2. Arsking, Erskine, De Cowey.
3. Alephe, Blund, Bosville, Brebner, Brem-

PLATE 92—*continued.*

ner, Cockain, Cokaine, Cokayne, Cooper, Fettiplace, Gideon, Giffard, Greet, Haggard, Heath, Law, Oakes, O'Connor, Reynolds, Seckford, Seckforde, Smallbrook, Tredcroft, Watkin, Wayneman, Wenman, White, Wyrall.
4. Dundas.
5. Ainsley, Ainslie, Bartram, Bruce, Bryce, Charingworth, Couper, Dale, Elliott-Fogg, Elliot, Erskine, Finlay, Guyling, Hadden, Halket, Hawling, Lindon, Macnamara, M'Rae, Martin, Ogilvie, Peachey, Richards, Strahan, Stratford, Vilo, Yawkins.
6. Aberbuthnet, Arbuthnot, Deale, Gulland, [illegible]im, Thomkins, Walker.
7. [illegible] Braham, Brende, De Blois, Etty, [illegible]ing, Mildmay, Mildway, Ogilvie, [illegible]ey, Waldron.
8. [illegible] Aljoy, Anketell, Auldjo, Belches, Belsches, Biset, Bisset, Bough, Bracebridge, Brasbridge, Crosbey, Crosbie, Cunninghame, Dalgleish, Fownes, Gregory, Hamilton, Horneck, Laurie, Lawder, Lawrie, Limesey, Mackenan, Mackeuan, Mackewan, M'Ewan, M'Lowe, Morton, Mottershed, Nairn, Plaine, Roddam, Scrogie, Smellet, Smollet, Tailefer, Trower, Watson, Wellwood.
9. Creveguer, Creverguere, Grant, Kirkpatrick, Mackenzie, M'Kenzie, M'Onald.
10. Coterell, Cotrell, Davers, Meurs, Mey, Plowman.
11. Aberbuthnot, Banaster, Banester, Chaffy, Comberford, De Montmorency, Griffiis, Mearns, Nanson, Pelham, Ridge, Snowden.
12. Braybrooke, Dagley, Goldston, Goldstone, Hoyles, Keys, Lessler, Lighton, Smith, Wolverstone.
13. Barban, Barbon, Beilby, Braine, Charleton, Charlton, Covert, Dennis, Dent, Godfrey, Hayes, Honby, Jeddon, Kymer, Lade, Leversedge, Little, Martyn, May, Michael, Michall, Michell, Paul, Pickering, Price, Taylour, Touke, Trivett, Warwick, Welford, Welsford, Wilsford.
14. Atfield, Bowdler, Clerke, Collis, Coult, Gemmel, Harris, Headfort, Mackenzie, M'Culloch, M'Kenzie, Montalt, Nibbs, Pickford, Taylor, Tuite, Young.
15. Ambrey, Ambry, Bath, How, Monteith.

PLATE 93.

1. Neale-Burrard.
2. Neweke,
3. Le Neve, Neave, Neeve, Neve.
4. Dunn, O'Dunn.
5. Down, Garstin, Hamerton, Naesmith, Nasmyth, Neasmith.
6. O'Hanlan.
7. Oldershaw.
8. Douglas, Nelthorpe, Russell.
9. Alwyn, Overbery, Overbury.
10. Oxborough, Oxburgh.
11. Nightingale.
12. Carnac, Carnac-Rivett, O'Mullen.
13. Betham, Davy, Knowles, Kyrby, Palmer, Pelly, Petty, Petye, Sanders, Villettes.
14. O'Donel.
15. Baptista, Palmes.

PLATE 94.

1. Arthur, Eden, Glemham, Hamby, Hansard, Oliphant, Pawlett, Shawe, Simpson, Smyth, Throckmorton, Twedy, Yate.
2. Avagour, Avaugour, Avougour, Curran, Curren, Hartford, Hertford, Knowell, Turtle.
3. Ash, Bressey, Breyton, Huskisson, Kennedy, May, Provis, Rutherford, Treswell.
4. Anwill, Anwyl, Culchech, Culcheth, House, Kiloh, Killowe, Myreton, Spence.
5. Ashburnham, Ayliffe, Burton, Byrom, Owens, Tankard, Telfer, Threlle.
6. Anstice, Anstis.
7. Blundell, Boterwike, Fownes, Gauler, Grogan, Hatton.
8. Bothwell, Boynell, Boyville, Hankin.
9. Bogg, Bouge, Colwich, Norrington, Novelle, Randall, Randolfe, Wakefield, Yellowley.
10. Blanchmaynes, Blanckmaynes, Brewsted, Brewster, Burnham, Carnegie, Chesterton, Collar, Cooke, Dennis, Fish, Gervis, Heddle, Jermyn, Joanes, Jones, Kymer, Lawson, Lutwyche, Mannock, Martin, Parnham, Paul, Paull, Pawle, Pinchyon, Pipe, Plantney, Pountney, Sheffield, Woodward.
11. Bicknall, Bicknell, Boughey Falconer, Hoddar, Hodder, Keith-Falconer, Sheridan.
12. Barlow, Bride, Kirkley, Kirkly, Wallace.
13. Cockes, Mayner, Minors, Mynords, Rowed, Shattock, Tawke.
14. Brickdale, Geoghegan, Luson, Maxfield, Shilton, Stannard.
15. Brome, Broom, Broome,

PLATE 95.

1. Maudevile, Napier, Treys.
2. Bayen, Cockett, Grandson, Shackleton, Shakelton.
3.
4. Grammer, Killegrew.
5. Mason, Morrison, Murison.
6. Beavan, Twicket.
7. Rolle.

PLATE 95—*continued.*

8. Botatort, Botetourt.
9. Amerie, Aynscomb, Eley, Elly, Iley, Nelson, Wood, Wynn.
10. Maxwell, Penniecook, Pennycuick.
11. Brocton, Buchanan, Gaven, Gawen, Sainsbury.
12. Hatsell.
13. M'Call, Mackauly.
14. Kinsey.
15. Aicken, Aickin, Forrester, Maltrevers, Russell.

PLATE 96.

1. Jutting.
2. Joye.
3. Jordan.
4. Castlecomb, Johnson.
5. Jones
6. Baker, Carlton, Carrie, Cleghorn, Cubit, Cubitt, Downing, Godbold, Hales, Hutcheson, Hutchison, Proudfoot, Rivers, Warren.
7. Hutchinson-Synge, Marchmont, Singe, Synge.
8. Huttoft.
9. Hughes.
10. Hay-Dalrymple.
11. Howe.
12. Brandling, Guilford.
13. Gremiston,
14. Gregory, Wheatling, Whitteley.
15. Greer.

PLATE 97.

1. Anderdon, Anderton, Armstrang, Armstrong, Johnston, Johnstone, Levy, Malmaynes, Murray, Partrick, Patrick.
2. Buller, Gleame, Maniot, Mauley, Moore, Quadring, Weldone.
3. Ayscough.
4. Aprece, Asloum, Colbroke, Colebrook, Colebrock, Hamilton, Mackinnon, Rankin, Town, Towne.
5. Beasley.
6. Askeby, Askely, Asklaby, Asklakby, Asklakeby, Aslakby, Aslakeby, Boyd, Cuppage, M'Indoe.
7. Beauchatt, Morvile.
8. Beesley, Beesly, Beseley, Besley, Besly, Lang, Langan, Winterbottom.
9. Beston, Bestoricke, Bestorike, Dawson, Dunning, Linwood, Taylor, Waters.
10. Champney, Evatt, Vaughan.
11. Balfour, Watts.
12. Cheeseman, Chesman, Glasgow, M'Robertson, Patmer, Robertson, Robison, Wallpool.
13. Chancy.
14. Blick, Blicke, Harold, Harrold, Keith, Leukenor, Wingfield, Wowan.
15. Bownes, Brews, Brewis, Charlesworth, Downie, Farmer, Fergushill, Goldington, Groves, Ogilby, Fermor, Witmore.

PLATE 98.

1. Child-Villiers, Cosson, Cossen, Cowan, Fitchett, Gerard, Lyddel, Manderne, Pates, Pauncefote, Villers, Villiers.
2. Cumberland, Hallwell, Halwell, Halywell, Vanneck, Van-Neck.
3. Amson, Panellee.
4. Vine.
5. Filbut, Filbutt, Green, Steer.
6. Promoli.
7. Feild.
8. Burge, Finlay, Hagell, Hamilton, Murray, Murry, Plank, Planke, Rusted, Somery, Tothill.
9. Fell, Hoe, Hoo, Lang.
10. Brenton, Fairfield, Hawkins, Hollyland, Holyland, O'Kelly.
11. Greenfield, Staveley.
12. Garrock, Gorges, Hodgson, Hook, Ord, Pike, Salmond, Saresbery.
13. Gainsby, Greenlees, Greenless.
14. Chadock, Chadwick, Darnley, Hackote, Jeffrey, Murray, O'Sullevan, Purfield, Pury, Tandy, Temple, Washington, Woryndon.
15. Arfece, Arfois, Arforce, Fellowes, Fellows, Grey, Strover, Trowtback, Williams-Lloyd.

PLATE 99.

1. Adam, Balsillie, Barber, Burn, Costley, Cromie, Dene, Drayton, Figgins, Francklin, Gerwood, Lint, M'Clesh M'Donald, Rattary, Rattray, Rowe, Seabrook, Shepheard, Shepperd, Sheridan, Taylor, Thomson, Warcop, Wickenden.
2. Acotis, Acottis, Acotts, Hugo, Hurell, Hurle, Hurrell, Muschamp.
3. Adams, Capper, Castle.
4. Baliol, Baylol, Cor, Meek, Meik.
5. Balmano, Balmanno.
6. Bareu, Barew, Barnet, Bland, Burnet, Irvine, Niven, Strickland, Walkfare, Wilkes.
7. Bendyshe, Campion, Cramer, D'Eureux, Devereux, Evreux, Gosell, Gossell, Harrison, Southouse, Wolseley.
8. Campbell, Dinwordy, Donnike, Drummond,

PLATE 99—*continued.*

Hamilton, Eliot, Elliott, Ferguson, Fitz-Hamon, Harbin, Lockhart-Elliott, Lowis, Neilson, Nelson, Onion, Puckle, Remington, Scot, Slesser, Swan, Walsh, Watkins, Winch, Winche, Yeomans.

9. Atfoe, Atsoe, Bec, Beck, Boustead, Canton, Docksey, Hamer, Henry, Home, Lyons, Peers, Sheridan, Sheriden, Wren.
10. Couchtree, Darlston, Gill, Gyll, Hatt, Hawkins, Jervis, Molynes.
11. Benson, Coles, Cossar, Cosser, Danrey, Daudie, Fulthorp, Fulthorpe, Gillow, Murray, Osevain, Rideout, Tory, Torry, Trotter, Vivian, Vyvyan.
12. Davey, Delamote, Delamotte, Smith, Tryon, Vass.
13. Borthwick, Davell, Dawson, Eglefelde, Eglefield, Luudin, Mather, Mein, Redege, Ridge.
14. Barker, Du Port, Kerdeston, Vine, Wescombe.
15. Adenstoun, Adingstoun, Adinston, Anby, Anbly, Aubley, Barber, Bennet, Boyes, Corben, Corbin, Corbyn, Edwards, Egmanton.

PLATE 100.

1. Ailesbury, Wiseman.
2. Abercorn, Boyne, Gray, Hamilton, Hamilton-Douglas.
3. Abercrombie, Abercromby, Bathgate, Beatson, Betson, Brandram, Byres, Congalton, Congalton, Connel, Connell, Dunfermline, Fettes, Fettew, Fitz-Pen, Gentle, Innes, Maher, Maxton, Meryon, Stewart, Tibbitts, Tuthill.
4. Aberdeen, Archer, Archever, Bower, Butters, Chipnan, Drummond, Fletcher, Flaxney, Gordon, Higgenbottom, Higginbottom, Hunter, Wasey.
5. Aberbuthnot, Arbuthnot, Bew, Currell, Gauden, Goodison, Hampden, Kidwell, Sankey, Tisdale, Tisdâll, Waltham.
6. Cotter, Garvey, Yelverton.
7. Gaynes,
8. Leicester, Parry, Rogers.
9. Blaydes, Halgoet.
10. Abdy, Abbey, Andlaw; Armory Company, Kerry; Aubrey, Baird, Banks, Baxter, Bruce, Campbell, Challeng, Cheoke, Dallender, Davie, Delawar, Diggs, Dikens, Divie, Divvie, Dyges, Dykes, Elfe, Elingham, Elphe, Golofer, Golston, Gorm, Gorrie, Gorrey, Graham, Haffenden, Keme, Kynn, M'Leod, Murray, Oughton, Rawlinson, Redhead, Richards, Roberts, Rollston, Rosher, Ross, Sideserf, Sidserf, Smithers, Sydserfe, Syme, Vaulx, Webster, Westhorpe, Whishaw.
11. Aboat, Abbot, Bayley, Clamond, Collee, Creevey, Crevy, Croft, Dolben, Fotheringham, Godwyn, Gooden, Gooding, Goodwin, Goodwyn, Hales, Halse, Halsey, Hobhouse, Howales, Loveney, M'Craw, Mulsho, Mulshoe, Norton, Palmer, Pardoe, Paston, Payton, Peiton, Pennel, Peyton, Pleasance, Steers, Sweetman, Worley.
12. Alvanley, Arden, Courtney, Waldegrave.
13. A'Beckett, Ateste, Becket, Beckett, Bennet, Blondevill, Blonville, Bosvargus, Busvargus, Cornewall, Cornish, Cornwall, Elmore, Fitz-Hewe, Fitz-Hugh, Foulerton, Gouldsmith, Heller, Hood, Kirwan, Ledsam, Mahewe, Mayow, Moore, Morgan, Parlar, Pearce, Pechell, Piper, Plumerdon, Rashleigh, Scarisbrick, Slingsby, Smallbones, Spaight, St. Quenton, Taunton, Tonkin, Wallis.
14. Anderson, Clunie, De Ponthieu, Monteith, Moorside, Murray, Paver, Ramsay.
15. Collins, Pegler.

PLATE 101.

1. Austavill, Boyce, Boyse, Cosars, Harley, Jane, Lepton, Lexton, M'Kellar, Parscoe.
2. Airlie.
3. Anncey, Austen, Austin, Clark, Ellwood, Flattesbury, Fleeming, Knight, Prescott, Skipton, Whitelaw.
4. Archer, Brawne, Mayne, Rea, Ree, Rider, De Rythrie, Surtees, Wright.
5. Byngham.
6. Amond, Ashton, Ayson, Bythesea.
7. Benweil, Benwell, Burghley, Burgly, Frampton, Mashiter.
8. Balasyse, Barnaby, Barneby, Bellasis, Bellassis, Cary, Christian, Cocker, Hughes, M'Kenzie.
9. Benton, Clack, Grose, Hyde, Pascall, Rowan.
10. Cookes, Gordon, Grantham, Mackie, M'Clambroch.
11. Berners, Fitz-Zimon, Gerard, Harris, Hays, Middleton, Scott, Zymon.
12. Bertrand, Bladford, Blandford, Hesding, Hislope, Port, Porte, Semple.
13. Gascoyne-Cecil, Tillet, Tillett.
14. Calley, Caley, Cayley.
15. Bock, Cawodly, Cawoodley, Copenger, Sapy, Sapye, St. Maur.

PLATE 102.

1. Coultnan, Crakenthorp, Ducket, Millar.
2. Bussell, Ducat, Duchet.
3. Broon, Dudgeon, Irvine.
4. Allan, Allen, Alleyn, Altham, Allyn, Alltham, Doe, Franks, Lamborn, Lamborne, Penwarne.

PLATE 102—*continued.*

5. Allot, Allott, Dodgin, Gillingham, Wright.
6. Dolphin, Dolphine.
7. Emmet, Emmett, Fourdrinier, Ham, Hamme, Tennant.
8. Eynes, Heynes.
9. Comyns, Crake, Fairford, Hosier, Lawrance, Micklethwaite.
10. Bevans, Bevains, Bloyam, Bloxham, Boddicott, Bodicote, Bodycoat, Keep, Swinford, Webster.
11. Askew, Ascough, Blommart, Bolron, Flude, Longley, M'Clelland.
12. Breche, Broderip, Brodrepp, Brodribb, Croker, Ferns, Whetnall.
13. Boot, Boote, Frome, Kenney.
14. Bassett, Basset, Beathell, Benwin, Bethell, Boulthee, Boultbie, Bradston, Bradeston, Bythell, Davies, De Pearsall, Erdeswike, Freeman, Lydcotte, Mount-Sandford, Norwood, Polstrod, Postlethwaite, Prescod, Prescot, Rand, Rande, Sandford, Smith, Stafford, Thirwell, Vincent, Wills-Sandford, Woodward, Wrottesley.
15. Bosne, Bosney, Broomhead, Brunet, Buggen, Buggin, Buggine, Daunt, Duckett, Fairbrother, Jessope, Maginn, Winstanley.

PLATE 103.

1. Atkinson, Hildershaw, Jeane, Loch, Lock, Spark, Sparke.
2. Beltoft, Beltofts, Limsay, Limsey.
3. Brudenell, Clarke, Coyne, Dansie, Jenkinson, Lancaster, Potter.
4. Bundy, Hynd, Jervy, Napier, Ryuell.
5.
6. Jermingham, Jerningham, Smyth.
7. Jockel.
8. Isaac.
9. De Grey, Hunloke, Kydermaster, Pilcher, Unett.
10. Jernegan.
11. Boreham, Borham, Borehont, Granville, Johns, Roffey, Tudor.
12. Jebb.
13. Ury.
14. Johnston.
15. Vach.

PLATE 104.

1. Allwright, Alwright, Brownlow, Chesterfield, Hard, Langmore, Parker.
2. Aubert.
3. Almewake, Alnwick, Blond, Laing, Nutt, Theobald.
4. Bishopston, Bishopstone, Bowen.
5. Bromflet, Bronslet.
6. Bidwell, Bydewell, Drummond, Hawkey, Oliver.
7. Brabant, Gaynsford, Gaynsforth, Hearne, Spear.
8. Botreaulx, Botreaux, Dellee, Flitt, Meggison, Tot, Wilcox.
9. Bradby, Holcomb, Holcombe, Lees.
10. Barnard, Bearcroft, Behevens, Berens, Betton, Betune, Clock, Cloke, Couch, Couche, Dehaney, Denhany, Grance, Hatton, Hornsby, Ludlow, Lymesey, Lyndsey, Nettleship.
11. Ayre, Bushnell, Hepworth, Innes, Melborne, Sault, Strachan, Strahan, Vezay, Vezey, Victor.
12. Close, Closs, Keating, Keeking.
13. Coblegh, Cobleigh, Cobley, Nowlan, Teasdale.
14. Clinch, Clynch.
15. Byngley, Bynley, Cope, Critchley, Critchlow, Derwell, Flanders, Harper, Hilliar, Lakinleech, Lakinlich, Letch, M'Whirter, Manston, Rose, Ross, Rosse, Whistler, Wills.

PLATE 105.

1. Aberkerdor, Aberkirdor, Aberkerdour, Dalziel, Barclay, Belean, Bonar, Blain, Blaine, Blane, Blean, Cazenove, Cornack, Currer, Dalziel, Deans, De Rinzy, Dymoke, Gowan, Hamilton, Justice, Osbourne, Poyntz, Roundell, Rundle, Scobie, Todrig, Vintris, Wells, Wemyss.
2. Broughton, Warberton, Warburton.
3. Cow, Cowee, Cowie, Cowey, Eagar, Paris.
4. Abercrombie, Ainsworth, Anesworth, Arthur, Atkinson, Bolton, Bowyer, Brabazon, Burrow, Carpenter, Chalmers, Chesham, Chirnside, Clagstone, Clark, Cleland, Congrave, Congreve, Cunliffe, Saumarez, Doig, Donavan, Donovan, Drummond, Eld, Ellicott, Hay-Carr, Falconer, Fifield, Frogmorton, Gargrave, George, Glenham, Halhead, Harding, Hawksworth, Henly, Holhead, Holme, Jenning, Jenny, Lanyon, Le Mesurier, Lowe, M'Crobie, Marsham, Maunsell, Meacham, Mitchelson, Moubray, Mowbray, O'Meaghir, Ormsby, Orrock, Pape, Partington, Paton, Patton, Pattone, Pepe, Pole, Pool, Poole, Price, Read, St. Aubyn, Saint-John, Shaw, Slaughter, Sterne, Straiton, Straton, Throckmorton, Throgmorton, Willes, Willis.
5. Fallowfield, Fitzroy, Grafton, Heming, Hemming, Gordon-Lennox.
6. Gabb, Keyes.
7. Abcot, Abcott, Adderly, Aiton, Aitoune, Aimes, Anketel, Annand, Annandale, Bogle, Brown, Buchanan, Cheisly,

PLATE 105—*continued.*

Chesly, Chiesly, Clelland, Dunbar, Dunlop, Gairden, Garden, Grubham, Janssen, Learmont, Learmonth, Lethoop, Liddel, Marmion, Mushet, Pinkerton, Rose, Ross, Vanheck, Whitham, Yorstone.
8. Abbot, Galay, Billers, Carpenter, Gilbertson, Kingsbuby.
9. Butts, Cairne, Garvine, Gibbens, Gibbins, Grayley, Grelley, Haddock, Hollier, Peat.
10. Delaland, Deland.
11. Babington, Brent, Browne, Castleton, Codrington, Coxwell, Dalton, Kenmare, Mann, Massinberd, Massingberd, Poynings, Wakefield.
12. Abelon, Abilon, Agard, Wroughton.
13. Bertie, Jack.
14. Anthony, Antonie, Antony, Bover, Bushe, Candler, Crawfurd, Dayrell, Flemming, Greatorex, Jackson, Kingsley, Kiviliock, Lamplugh, Leveson, Loggie, Morton, Oddy, Pyne, Ruthven, Tims, Waller.
15. Botell, Bothell, Coryton, Kay, Lisle, Ogilvie, Rand, Randes.

PLATE 106.

1. Aylett.
2. Thicknesse.
3. Awborn, Goucell, Osborne, Osbourne.
4. Athwat.
5. Audin, Giddy.
6. Adderley, Atherley, Dale.
7. Astell.
8. Attelounde, Attelound.
9. Arnold, Wingham.
10. Byne.
11. Ashley, Astley.
12. Byerly, Byerley, Byorley.
13. Byam, Price, Thomas.
14. Arney.
15. Botteler, Butler.

PLATE 107.

1. Beaumont, Cheeke, Ellis, Kinerby, Love, Magrath, Paddye, Talbot.
2. Conelly, Connelly, Conolly, Montgomerie.
3. Billing, Billinge, Germain.
4. Bomford, Cromuel, Graham, Guthrie, Road, Roades.
5. Bayons, Bayos, Benningham, Colt, Rowles.
6. Burdet, Burdett, Lorand, Warde, Wickham.
7. Burgoyne, Colne, Colney, Gessors, Ghrimes, Hoofsteller, Horne, Hunt, Norris, Plumbe, Sturges, Temple, Topliffe, Toplis.
8. Lawson.
9. Codd, Codde, Long.
10. Bagenhall, Bagnall, Beke, Caulfield, Hall, Reeves, Reve.
11. Burgone, Burgoyne, Condie, Goodhard, Goodhart, Hames, Haycock, Howston, Wedgewood.
12.
13. Abercromby, Abram, Harnet, Hartwell.
14. Duckworth, Scot, Scott.
15. Pennel, Pennell, Reddie, Walsh.

PLATE 108.

1. Alford.
2. Alfrey, Allfrey.
3. Allen.
4. Amary, Dawson.
5. Allen, Allin, Partridge.
6. Babington.
7. Baddiford.
8. Alsop.
9. Bacon.
10. Baldock.
11. Amo.
12. Bales.
13. Bancroft, Ferne, Middleton.
14. Baker, Mortimore.
15. Banks.

PLATE 109.

1. Caster, Clermont, Gabell, Gallicz, Gellie, Gelly.
2. Amycot, Amyatt, Arbuckle, Battersbee, Battersby, Blossome, Blossun, Budds, Elliot, Elliott, Gage, Kershaw, Manwell, Rawlings, Shepheard, Staple, Stenynge, Yea.
3. Ballward, Balvaird, Blaverhasset, Bryson, Burn, Forrester, Hacklet, Hackluit, Limborne.
4. Farrow, Gerbridge, Haddow, Hadlow, Harrington, Jay, Kempster, Scot, Underwood.
5. Burton, Edwards, Favill, Holliday, Idle, Olivier, Poingdestre, Sciaualuga, Shekell, Stokely, Street, Tillard, Twigg, Twigge, Tyron, Walleys, Wigmore.
6. Innes.
7. Cooper, Gavin, Hanbury.
8. Abernethy, Abernethy, Anderson, Arbuthnot, Asche, Ascher, Aschey, Asher, Baird, Bennet, Bogle, Brown, Bryson, Cairnie, Camel, Constable, Delamare, Duncan, Edmonds, French, Gall, Gordon, Heppell, Hyghlord, Jameson, Jamieson, Knevet, Knight, Leyham, Mont-

PLATE 109—*continued.*

chency, Moreland, Mudie, Murray, O'Maly, Poulter, Schardelow. Quatherine, Rankine, Scot, Scott; South Sea Company; Stackhouse, Stephenson, Stirling, Strachan, Suttie, Tendering, Tendring, Tompkins, Watson, Whitton, Wood.

9. Abberbury, Bradford, Burgis, Butter, Campbell, Carron, Clove, Clynch, Columball, Darwen, Darwin, Edmiston, Edmistone, Eldres, Fordyce, Fullarton, Kahl, Lockwood, M'Gilvray, Palley, Stother, Stutville, Sutherland, Wheeler, Wheler, Woodburne, Woodthorpe.
10. Brock, Corby, Edgell, Harrison, Kandishe, Longden, Swynerton.
11. Crookshank, Prest.
12. Bonniman, Gib, Johnson, Johnston, Knight, Langmead, Lofthouse, Wailes, Wiggins.
13. Fitz-Henry, Immans, Inmans, Mabball, Mabbatt, Maule.
14. Crowder, Heigham, MacArthur, Main.
15. Aguillon, Atkins, Borthwick, Bromhead, Buckston, Buxton, Clavedon, Culverton, Fell, Ffytche, Forbes-Leith, Gauldesborough, Hartop, Hendry, Hume, Jegon, Keir, Lechmere, Leechman, Leeshman, Leverton, Meadows, Mears, De Medewe, Mitchell, Moorhouse, Nash, O'Cuilean, O'Meara, O'Meard, Peterson, Peyrse, Rising, Steward, Stewart, Weatherhead.

PLATE 110.

1. Abbot.
2. Atton, Attone, Bradestone, Bradston, Bradstone, Bramwell, Dobyns, Royston.
3. Allnett, Allnutt, Almot, Alneot, Alnot, Cobbold, Hatchet, Hatchett, Hawley, Kennoway, Whitehead.
4. Blenerhasset, Blennerhasset, Blenerhassett, Bleverhasset, Buchan, Cudden, De La Fons, Kelk, Kelke, Plonckett, Plunkett, Webb, White, Yer.
5. Allingham, Kirkland, Kirkley, Land, Plesseis.
6. Boodle, Devon, Gwinnett, Hodgetts, Jaques, Price.
7. Abbot, Hibbert, Naper, Napier.
8. Bocking, Charlton, Delapoole, Knatchbull, Lewis, Montagu.
9. Butterworth, Fernandez, Hengham, Knolles.
10. Boleyn, Bolleyn, Boleyne, Bollens, Bollin, Boulby, Bowlby.
11. Bowditch, Bygot, Cron, Crone, Finney, Herbot, Thursby.
12. Bowley.
13. Agnew, Boyton, Leland, Murdoch, Silvester, Sylvester.
14. Bramson, Branson, Braunson, Cole, Colle, Crotty, Hinckes, Hincks, Hinks.
15. Bracey, Brassy, Finn, Fynmore, Manton.

PLATE 111.

1. Ashfield, De Bohun, Damory, Dogherty, Doherty, Folman, Garforth, Kaines, M'Carthy, Martindale, Qurrell, Smyth, Wolf, Wolfe.
2. Cowell, Dundas, Lacy.
3. Busterd, Cannon, Durham, Gwyn, Harliston, Lake, Leak, Maclaren, Munton, Todman, Willison.
4. Barnby, Berkeley, Berkley, Calcott-Berkeley, Cambell, Champayn, Chrisope, Cohen, Deane, Desborough, Desbrowe, Downing, Hall, Newton.
5. Adams, Aderston, Aderstone, Adderstone, Addreston, Anstay, Anstee, Anstey, Anstie, Anston, Ansty, Applebee, Argenton, Arundel, Asen, Audley, Audly, Bickerton, Bidwell, Bigot, Bigott, Binns, Bird, Blackwell, Blessone, Bostock, Caldecot, Camac, Camic, Cargill, Chadock, Chadwick, Chernock, Coe, Crimes, Crymes, Denton, Douglas, Drysdale, Fitzhugh, Forde, Fournier, Gawler; City of Glasgow; Glen, Glenn, Gossip, Gould, Greive, Grimes, Grive, Hansard, Hayman, Headley, Hedley, Hill, Hudson, Irwine, Isaac, Keene, Lessingham, Lusher, M'Aben, M'Carin, M'Cubbin, MacDeargan, M'Deargan, M'Gill, Mallabar, Martineau, Martyn, Monckton, Monketon, Moncton, Nuttall, Oulton, Owlton, Pickett, Pigot, Priest, Proctor, Rathlow, Reynell, Ridell, Riddell, Rutherford, Rutherfurd-Oliver, Sandford, Sanford, Smallbrook, Smith, Stott, Stringer, Strother, Tempest, Thomson, Torrens, Vandeleur, Vawdrey, Waddington, Walkingshaw, Waud, Weedon, Wiggon, Winter.
6. Bradley, Carrant, Crofts, Dougal, Gowshell, Havard, Johnson, Layfield, Lyfield, M'Cann, M'Leod, Mortimer, Turnbull, Venant, Vincent, Whitbroke, Wright.
7. Bowyer.
8. Calthrop, Naper, Napper.
9. Amson, Crane, Morphew, O'Brien, Ratcliff, Sleath, Storar, Storer.
10. Heard, Ochterlony.
11. Avery, Barnoby, Bootle, Donkin, Hinchley, Lenche, Packenham.
12. Hellen, Vandeput.
13. Airth, Andrews-Windsor, Calibut, Crosell, De Romara, De Romera, Estcourt, Godard, Goddard, Goddart, Gordon, Hickmann, Mantell, Northage, Wallpool, Walpole, Windsor.
14. Bartan, Bartane, Bartain, Bouwen, Carrol, Caroll, Dukes, Hartford, Lindsay, Marmyon, Quicke, Shed, Westlemore, Whitaker.
15. Bateman, Cooker, Cooper, M'Coll, Ramsay, Reynolds, Sandeland, Sandilands.

PLATE 112.

1. Forster.
2. Ewar.
3. Forrester.
4. Foulks.
5. Foster.
6. Fountbery, Meddowes, Meddus.
7. Eyre, Fraser, Smith.
8. Francklin, Franklin.
9. Giffard.
10. Godden, Littlefield, Oldfield, Ouldfield.
11. Freeman-Williams.
12. Goodsir.
13. Croone, Gray.
14. Fulwar.
15. Goldtrap.

PLATE 113.

1. Hamilton, Lewis.
2. Hammick.
3. Jervoise-Clarke, Mannock, Oliver.
4. Hamond.
5. Andrews, Jephson.
6. Beighton, Hampson.
7. Jefferyes.
8. Bourke, Hanmer, Roberts.
9. Jennerson.
10. Keith.
11.
12. Colson, Kelsey.
13. Kemble.
14. Johnson, Philimore, Walsh.
15. Alban, Kemor.

PLATE 114.

1. Bickerstaffe, Fead, Grey.
2. Braybroke, Braybrook. Norton.
3. Bartelott-Smyth, Bartlet, Bartlett, Barttelot, Smyth.
4. Beche, Dickenson, Norden.
5. Browne, Robottom, Robottan, Stones.
6. Bontein, Bonteine, Bunting; Company of Clockmakers; Collings, Freer, Gregory, Murray-Nairne, Pont.
7. Brignac, Clench, Clenche, De Carteret, Dowbiggin, Hardress, Malynes, Morgan, Newington.
8. Brownell, Fitzwilliam, Hankley, Harwood, Haule, Lambert, Scroop, Scroope, Scrope, Sheil, Stockdale.
9. Chevers, Dickens, Gerson, Kennett, Kenwick, Keryell, Toriano.
10. Adams, Drummond, Leybourne.
11.
12. Decker.
13. Kittermasten, Kydermaster, Marter, O'Donovan, Styles, Worden.
14. Corbet, Corbot, St. Paul.
15. Casey, Hargraves, Heyford, Heyforde, Montgomery, Neale, Neele.

PLATE 115.

1. Badger.
2. Bacon, Crochrod.
3. Bagnall.
4. Littlehales.
5. Baird, Campbell, Sinclair.
6. Camber.
7.
8. Balam.
9. Campbell, Constable, Maly.
10. Camper, Lysers.
11. Daunscourt.
12. Dalling.
13. Aldborough, Aldeburghe, Edwards, Inkeldon, Inkledon, Nightingall.
14. Alstantan, Bevereham, Bindley, Bindly, Cameron, Cooke, Deuchar, Franke, Macquaire, Maudis, Tatlock, Warley, Woorley, Worley.
15. Egerton.

PLATE 116.

1. Lamb.
2. Cavandish, Cavendish, Lagenham, Mole.
3. Lamb.
4. Bellismo, Horton, Lane.
5. Lambert.
6. Lambert, Sea, See.
7. Lambton-Dawson.
8. Atsley, Champney, Croughton, Gillson, Parker, Maidman; Muscovy Merchants; Poultney, Pulteney; Russia Merchant Company; Sparkling, Sugden, Taylor, Villet.
9. Lane.
10. M'Donald.
11. Callagan, O'Callagan, O'Callaghan, M'Donagh, M'Donogh.
12. Macdonald.
13. Macken.
14. Bridger, Burkin, Danby, Lowyn, M'Kaile.
15. Bevers, Brickenden, Croker, D'Oiley, D'Oyley, Lefray, M'Kirdy, Magin.

PLATE 117.

1. Saunders.
2. Salisbury.
3. Savage.
4. Barnard, Bottell, Bower, Brandreth, Brock, Brownell, Clarke, Cowan, Dealtry, Dishington, Frodsham, Froelsham, Graham, Hassard, King, Kingscote, Luke, Major, Mulholland, Murray, Pilgrime, Pringle, Prior, Pryer, Pryor, Samfoord, Schelley, Smith, Solomons, Strickland, Thyly.
5. Savignac.
6.
7. Tetlow.
8. Dawson, Sawyer.
9. Thackeray, Thackery.
10. Thorndike.
11.
12. Tomlins.
13. Venables.
14. Lucas, Scot, Scott, Sword, Swourd, Ventris.
15. Vansittart.

PLATE 118.

1. Laffer, Marker, Monke, Williams.
2. Kinnaird, Ladd, Ladde, Sandilands.
3. Athelstan, Athelston, Downton.
4. Bludworth, Breeton, Drummond-Burrel, Glaston, Landal, Landale, Landel, Landell, M'Kenzie, Melville-Whyte, Simpson, Stocken, Whytt.
5. Hawkins, Pocock.
6. M'Alla, M'Aulay, Mackauly.
7. Dangerfield, Ladkin, Livingstone, Muir, Multon, Mure, Napier, Ruck.
8. M'Cleod, M'Cloud, Mackloide.
9. Champerouon, Keirie, Loggie, Logy, M'Cartnay, M'Cartney, Macartney, Maccartney, MacKartney, Nechure, Paton, Peters, Rose, Ross, Sherwood, White.
10. Bartley, Carswell, Fischer, Ganuble, Napton, Reid, Talbot, Owers.
11. Dietz, Egg, Gibbines, Gibbins, Nassau, O'Donnel, O'Donnell.
12. Kaer, Lane, Lanis.
13. Bucke, Drought, Isherwood, Longstaff, Nettles, Swallow, Walker.
14. Lake, Preston, White.
15. Burnell, Castell, Castle, Crosse, Heath, Hopkins, Johnson, Kearney, Morris, Paddon.

PLATE 119.

1. Mardake.
2. M'Corda.
3. Allanson-Winn.
4. M'Gregor.
5. Macdonald, Saunders-Dundas.
6. M'Kenny.
7. Gillies, Gillis, Litton, Lowrie, Lowry, M'Intosh, M'Pherson, Pennington, Rae, Richard, Rickart.
8. Brudenal, Brudenell, Maclean, M'Lean.
9. Mallow.
10. Everard, Manford, Sutton.
11. Mallow.
12. Malton.
13. Martin.
14. Elham, Leath, Leatt, Marewood.
15. De Butts, Houlton, Maccaunach, Martin, Martyn, Taylour.

PLATE 120.

1. Armitage, Armstrong, Armytage, Fulkworth, Fuller, Gilmore, Gilmour, Heathfield, Keir, Lalor, Winstanley, Woodcock.
2. Furse, Ivory.
3. Andrew, Andrewes, Andrews, Annyslay, Blaikie, Borthwick, Du Halgoet, Fondre, Grosselin, M'Clelland, Macklellan, M'Lellan, Moir, More, Newborough, Pecksall, Pexall, Quadering, Seymour, Seymour, Shirley, Stirling, Weltden.
4. Dauntsey, Dickenson, Geale, Sabine, Westly.
5. Batson, Burrow, De Senlize, Eyre, Holbrook, Marshall, Muriell, Strange.
6. Begbie, Furnes, Furnese, Furness.
7. Aston, Bailwood, Bate, Baynham, Beamont, Beaumont, Beauvous, Bevil, Bilsland, Bissland, Bullsland, Bloomfield, Bodley, Bolaine, Boloine, Bolstrode, Brage, Bulkeley, Bulkely, Bullen, Cole, Colvile, Colvil, Colville, Crofts, Freke, Gore, Hastings, Hay, Horne, Houghton, James, Jenkinson, Lawler, Loxdale, Overy, Percehay, Porter, Ratcliffe, Richardson, Rudston, Ruxton, Sanford, Shoffield, Spayne, Tailbois, Tailboys, Thorpe, Whitney, Widdrington, Williams, Witherington, Wodrington.
8. Alington, Allington, Anderson, Barwell, Bell, Boniface, Broadley, Broughton, Cartiles, Chafin, Chaffin, Cheese, Clapperton, Cochet, Davers, Dawson, Edwards, Eure, Fall, Goche, Gooch, Grosvenor, Grovesnor, Haggerston, Haydon, Headon, Heydon, Linford, Lovell, M'Fadyen, M'Faiden, Panter, Penteland, Philip, Pointer, Porterfield, Rees, Russell, Sanderson, Saunderson, Saxon, Shaw, Sherington, Smith, Smyth, Stockdale, Stout, Swinnee, Swiney, Talbot, Temple, Thomas, Warren, Williams, Wyllie, Yea.
9. Aland, Ben, Benne, Clements, Ferrarils, Ferrers, Howland, Maddox.
10. Bromeall, Chater, Cowan, Leslie, Lesly, Lodge, Stokes, Storie, Stoto, Stuckey, Sutton.
11. Archideckine, Bellew, Bickerton, Camp-

PLATE 120—*continued.*

bell, Cantillion, Clayton, Colby, Conner, Douglas, Fay, Gaselee, Geogham, Grassal, Grassall, Greaves, Greive, Grieve, Kirkpatrick, Lemarch, Lysaght, M'Allister, M'Hud, Mahon, Montgomery, Mundell, Pasley, Preston, Radford, Ross, Schrieber, Vade.

12. Clere, Machell, Matchell, Merbury, Muchell, Pepys, Pipe.
13. Conyston, Eldridge, Iliff, Low, Maillard, Sherard, Sherrard, Shippard, Townsend.
14. Hanbury, Leigh-Hanbury, Wildman, Williams.
15. Howard.

PLATE 121.

1. Hawksworth, Hutton.
2. Kirkaldie, Kirkaldy, Maxwell, Newarke.
3. Gammell.
4. Aleston, Alston, Branscomb, Bronscomb, Fenning, More.
5. Andros, Beyard, Blithe, Bound, Bowker, Coles, Kerdiffe, Marleton, Middleton, Skearne, Skerne, Skryne.
6. Brackley, De Ferrars, Eddisbury, Ferrars, Stanley.
7. Aguilar, Aguillar, Walcot, Walcott, Woolcot.
8. Appleford, De Montgomery, White.
9. Bridger, Briger, Budd, Coldham, Fitz-Thomas, Neale, Pemberton.
10. Alderford.
11. Cooke, Dunsford, Stratton, Umfrevile, Umphreville, Wilmot.
12. Andrea.
13. Lumisden, Lumsdean, Solomon.
14. Argall, Dakyns, Dawson, Farrand, Ferrand, Gibbs, Gilson, Gull, Gytties, Hagley, Halke, Hall, Jackson, Jeremy, Joyner, Lawson, Leveson, Leye, Ludlow, Mayney, Nevett, Nunn, Polkinghorne, Rattray, Samler, Whitter, Worklych, Wright.
15. Saxby.

PLATE 122.

1. Courteis, Curteis, Curtess, Curteys, Curtois, Curtoys, Dracelow, Drakelow, Duckenfield, Hay, Hay-Drummond, Mahon, Wardrop, Wardrope.
2. Copildike, Copledike, Copledyke, Sommerville.
3. Bunten, Bunting, Churchman, Cocksey, Cookesey, Cooksey, Coventry, Gerney, Jopp, Wyman.
4. Crakenthorpe, Craufurd, Crawford, Kirch, Looker, Lyndown, Ufflete.
5. Cornwallis, Fitz-Rause.
6. Cron, Crone, Ged, Gedd, Geddes, Geddies, Toby.
7. Crews, Crewse, Cruse.
8. Aylward, Cowcey, Cowcie, Cowey, Sexton.
9. Cubit, Cubitt, Dowse, Graham.
10. Cowling, Holmes, Homan, Lovis, Machen, Machin, Maze.
11. Brereton, Collin, Collins, Craven, Granville, Greenfield, Umpton, Upton.
12. Biest, Brampston, Crucks, Greerson, Greir, Grier, Gresoun, Grierson, Ingles, Lockhart.
13. Crockat, Crockett, Dand, Fazakerley, Guest, Patton.
14. Athell, Cropley, Linch, Salkyns.
15. Crawford, Durham, Hay, Innes, Kyd, Mitchelson, Monins, Monyns, Pettegrew, Ramage.

PLATE 123.

1. Archbald, Archibald, Hastie, Innes, Keir, Lithgow, Montgomery, Paterson, Porterfield, Small, Thompson, Tompson.
2. Adams, Averinges, Beynham, Cawthorne, Coringham, Coryngham, Craister, Craster, Crook, Damboys, Gatacre, Kirwan, Mackie, M'Kie, Mackie, M'Morran, Protheroe, Raven, Rice, Rokeby, Rook, Rookby, Shearwood.
3. Agnew, Durban, Grant, Shadford, Shadforth, Streveling, Traquair, Travers.
4. Bamford, Baumford, Baunford, Horncastle, Knight, Vivian.
5. Barr, Christie, Colquhon, Colquhoun, Duer, Massingbird, Mathison, Melhuish, Murray, Ross, Sprigg, Weller.
6. Band, Desse, Fowler, Hawkes, Hudson, Humble, Nicholas, Snell.
7. Cane, Glasier, Glazier, Hamilton.
8. Camville, Curtayne, Raymond.
9. Ady, Adry, Austie, Cantelow, Cooley, Dawbeney, Leversedge, Prestwick, Tenison, Watkins.
10. Burket, Burkett, Burkitt, Chauncey, Davis, Downham, Erskine, Laleman, Leaver, Leckie, Lecky, Raynes, Westwood, Wilton.
11. Darrell, Du Mouline, Walley.
12. Barney, Blackwall, Bremner, Brymer, Carmichael, Chape, Chappe, Chappes, Darling, Fillingham, Kerby.
13. Egremond.
14. Allingridge, Ashborne, Ashburne, Bartlelot, Beseley, Capsal, Capsall, Copland, Copeland, Coppland, Cowpland, Elkins, Hunt, Lilborne, Lilbourne.
15. Aselock, Aslake, Aslack, Asloke, Baron, Barrel, Barrell, Bonest, Bonus, Bower, Bowre, Bukhill, Carter, Chitty, Colvil, Colville, Elkins, Ellerker, Forsham, Freston, Gamell, Gammel, Gamonill, Hall, Harrington, Haselden, Hasle-

PLATE 123—*continued.*

tine, Hastaline, Highmore, Hull, Lace, Lambeth, M'Donald, M'Kellip, Melveton, Malvile, Melville, Melville, Moutrie, Ogilvie, Powell, Robins, Tirringham, Turbutt, Walcher, Wedderburn-Colvile.

PLATE 124.

1. Barham, Barnardiston, Peart, Pert, Thaker.
2. Barkeman, Barkham.
3. Barlow.
4. Cardigan.
5. Barnard.
6. Carlos, Hopper.
7. Caryer.
8. Bartram.
9. Cervington.
10. Burnet, Burnett, Christie, Dawbency.
11. Bateman.
12. Anderson, Church, De Bouche, Kempton.
13. Duxbury.
14. Chapman.
15. Dymoke, Dymock.

PLATE 125.

1. Bennet, Upton.
2. Paske, Whicker.
3. Van Voorst.
4. Clunes, Hill, Ogle, Poynes.
5. Ap-Howell, Blaw, Cleather, Cruikshank, Delap, Fane, Fay, Fergus, Fleming, Gee, Hartagan, Hartigan, Vane-Stewart, Luther, Lyell, M'Nore, Meverell, Montgomery, Parker, Philips, Pinkton, Richardson, Rivett, Slater, Smallman, Vane.
6. Wadham.
7. Hill, Oglethorpe, Wall.
8. Waldesheecheff, Waldesheff, Waldaheff.
9. Walmouth.
10. Marsh, Yester.
11. Walford.
12. Yong.
13. Young.
14. Walker.
15. Younge.

PLATE 126.

1. Adyn, Boswell, Boughton, Burdett, Chambers, Cooke, Davies, Dundas, Ellis, Fairlie, Fairly, Gisland, Glin, Goodrich, Gort, Grassick, Lisle, Loane, Mascy, Masey, Masey, Maude, Morris, Moston, Munn, Peak, Pedley, Pine, Pirce, Ridsdale, Rowsewell, Rowswell, Stewart, Whitington, Whittingham, Whyte, Wilson, Wittingham.
2. Alland.
3. Ames, Amos.
4. Cavenagh, Coulthurst, Jago, Lear, Watson.
5. Asherst, Ashurst, Blaney, Blayney, Brigges, Fox, Kirkenton, Pierpont, Pierrepoint, Pierrepont, Reynell, Ross, Staunton.
6. Annesley, Grandison.
7. Atkinson, Aubyn, Burche, Burrough, Borough, Clark, Clogston, Curle, Curson, Daulbeny, Dudley, Gloag, Jarrat, Jarret, Jeggings, Jegon, Lacey, Langtree, Ludkin, M'Andrew, Macgregor, Maher, Marley, Milborne, Morton, Munro, Niblet, Nisbet, Richards, Schank, Simpson, Streeter, Ypres.
8. Spendluff, Stapleton, Touchet.
9. Bellairs, Bellars, Boothby, Bromley, Buchanan, Carmarden, Carmarthen, Deane, Dodington, Dumas, Dundas, Goldingham, Gouldingham, Harnage, Hurry, Kennard, Livesay, Livesey, M'Dougal, M'Dowal, M'Dowall, Magnus, Mills, Morton, Newcom, Newcombe, Newcome, Newdigate, Ogilvie, Pegg, Penton, Pickering, Pole, Powel, Powell, Pridham, Prudhome, Prudon, Rae, Rotherfield, Savage, Thorley, Ure, Urrie, Urry, Walter, Wellesley-Pole, Wetherton, Wheterton, Whitehouse, Whitmarsh, Wilney, Wilson, Worrall.
10. Adye, Adyer, Ambrose, Brady, Bushell, Busshell, Bussell, Carruthers, Clavering, Courtney, Desanges, Donhault, England, Foggo, Fogo, Jellicoe, Legat, Leggatt, Lugg, Menzies, Murray, Overend, Porter, Sarjeantson, Wood.
11. Blackney, Blackeney, Blakeny, Colter, Coulter, Morrell, Trimnel, Trimnell.
12. Bennet, Bent, Beswick, Chubbe, Compere, Hallet, Purchas, Rous, Rouse.
13. Davies.
14. Bethune, Burdenbroke, Fullarton, Hately, Holmden, Holmeden, Kellam, Kellum, Kinnard, Lindsay, Merks.
15. Blithe, Bond, Bonde, Chamonde, Elvet, Eyston, Fell, Green, Hanman, Kempthorne, Lee, Legatt, Le Hunt, Ley, Salmon, Shershall, Silly.

PLATE 126*a*.

1. Allestry, Arrol, Duff, Ferguson, Jeffery, Kukefield, Meek, Newton, Scepter.
2. M'Connel.
3. Ratcliff.
4. Nimmo.
5. M'Connel.
6. Conolly, Dixon.
7. Charley, Chorley.

PLATE 126 *a—continued.*

8. Flockhart.
9. Gordon, Mercer, Millar, Ral, Ralph, Reid, Salthouse.
10. Crompe, Grant, Macpherson, M'Bean.
11. Gurney.
12. Gurney.
13. Bulmar, Edmondson, Gibbons, Ile, Isaacson, Isle, James, Loane, Maskelyne, Shiers, Standbridge, Taylor.
14. Baynes.
15. Chadwick.

PLATE 126 *b.*

1. Newenham.
2. Weir.
3. Greig.
4. Pilkington.
5. Clark.
6. Vivian.
7. Lindsay.
8. Webb.
9. Kenney.
10. Miles.
11. Nugent.
12. Horsford.
13. Gulston.
14. Northmore.
15. Brocas.

PLATE 126 *c.*

1. Lee.
2. Phillipps.
3. Macalester.
4. Horsfall.
5. Turnor.
6. Harrison.
7. Smyth-Pigott.
8. Watson.
9. Marche, Phillipps.
10. Ettrick.
11. Hughes.
12. M'Murray.
13. Pigott, Smyth.
14. Norwood.
15. Omond.

PLATE 126 *d.*

1. Haworth.
2. Walker.
3. Pownall.
4. Thompson.
5. Tower, Baker.
6. Close.
7. Russel.
8. Worth, Newenham.
9. Gray.
10. Baker.
11. Patrick.
12. Ralston, Patrick.
13. Bankes.
14. Moss.
15. Turton.

PLATE 127.

BRITISH CROWNS AND CORONETS, REGALIA OF ENGLAND, &c.

Fig.

1. Prince of Wales' Coronet.
2. Royal or Imperial Crown.
3. Coronet for younger Sons and Brothers of the Blood Royal.
4. Coronet for Nephews of the Blood Royal.
5. Coronet for Princess Royal and younger Sisters.
6. Duke's Coronet.
7. Marquis's Coronet.
8. Earl's Coronet.
9. Viscount's Coronet.
10. Archbishop's Mitre.
11. Baron's Coronet.
12. Bishop's Mitre.
13. Cap of Dignity or Maintenance; also called a chapeau.
14. St. Edward's Crown.
15. The Crown of State worn by King Charles II.
16. The King's Coronation Ring.
17. Golden Sceptre.
18. Sceptre, called St. Edward's Staff.
19. Sceptre with the Dove.
20. Golden Orb or Mound.
21. Queen Mary's Sceptre.
22. Ivory Sceptre.
23. Broken Sword.
24. The Queen's Coronation Ring.
25. Crown of State.
26. The Queen's Circlet of Gold.
27. The Crown which the Queen wears on her return to Westminster Hall.

PLATE 128.

CROWNS, CORONETS, ORDERS, CHAPLETS, AND HELMETS.

1. Celestial Coronet or Crown.
2. Eastern or Antique Coronet.
3. Ducal Coronet.
4. Order of the Bath.
5. Crown worn by King Edward I.
6. Triumphal Crown or Garland.
7. King's Helmet.
8. Helmet of the Nobility.
9. Civic Crown.
10. Order of the Thistle.
11. Order of the Garter.
12. Order of St. Patrick.
13. Knight's Helmet.
14. Esquire's Helmet.
15. Obsidional Crown or Garland.
16. Chaplet.
17. Vallary Crown.
18. Mural Crown.
19. Naval Crown.
20. Hanoverian or Guelphic [Order.
21. Palisado Coronet.

PLATE 129.

FLAGS OF ALL NATIONS.

1. Prussia.
2. England.
3. Belgium.
4. Holland.
5. Hanover.
6. Colombia.
7. Sardinia.
8. Venitian Lombardy.
9. La Plata.
10. Switzerland.
11. France.
12. New Granada.
13. United States.
14. Brazil.
15. Mexico.
16. Bolivia.
17. Otahiti.
18. Buenos-Ayres.
19. Chili.
20. Peru.
21. Venezuela.
22. Russia.
23. Montevideo.

PLATE 130.

FLAGS OF ALL NATIONS—*continued.*

1. Poland.
2. Austria.
3. Hamburg.
4. Sweden.
5. Malta.
6. Greece.
7. Mecklenburg.
8. Norway.
9. Malabar.
10. Japan.
11. Denmark.
12. Portugal.
13. Spain.
14. Tunis.
15. Ionian Islands.
16. Arabia.
17. Morocco.
18. Turkey.
19. China.
20. Burmah.
21. Persia.
22. Tuscany.
23. Egypt.

PLATE 131.

SPECIMENS OF LETTERING, CRESTS, AND SCROLLS AND GARTERS WITH MOTTOES.

1. Old English. M.P.
2. Ornamental Initials, Cyphered. G.W.M.
3. Shaded Saxon. L.B.
4. Sprigged Script. C.W.
5. German Text. R.G.
6. Plain Initials, Cyphered. D.H.
7. Open Block. M.
8. Ornamental Print. R.
9. Ornamental Script. G.H.
10. Open German Text. T.A.L.
11. Ornamental Script, Cyphered. B.F.
12. Old English. C.H.
13. Old English. G.D.
14. Flowered Ornamental, Entwined. R.P.D.
15. Ornamental Script. A.R.
16. Ornamental Script. T.P.
17. Open Roman. B.
18. Black Roman. E.
19. Open Script. J.M.
20. Ornamental Script. W.T.
21. Italian Script. R.K.
22. Crest, Garter, and Motto.
23. Monogram, Crest, Scroll, and Motto.
24. Crest, Garter, Motto, and Initials.
25. Crest and Initials.
26. Coronet and reversed Initials entwined. L.D.
27. Monogram.
28. Crests, Scroll, and Motto.
29. Initials, reversed, Cyphered, Garter and Motto. E.H.B.
30. Initials and Crest.
31. Crest.

PLATES 132–140.

MONOGRAMS, OR REVERSED INITIALS.

PLATE 141.

HERALDIC ILLUSTRATIONS FOR CHARGINGS, &c.

PLATE 142.

FOREIGN CROWNS.

1. Imperial, French.
2. Pope.
3. France.
4. Spain.
5. Portugal.
6. Denmark.
7. Russia.
8. Grand Seignor.
9. Prussia.
10. Poland.
11. Charlemain.
12. Corsica.
13. Grand Duke of Tuscany.
14. Doge of Venice.
15. Arch Duke.
16. Brunswick.
17. Dauphin.
18. Electoral.

PLATE 143.

ARMS OF CITIES.

1. Liverpool. | 2. Dublin. | 3. London. | 4. Manchester. | 5. Aberdeen.

PLATE 144.

ARMS OF CITIES, &c.

1. Edinburgh. | 2. Regalia of Scotland. | 3. Birmingham. | 4. Sheffield.

TITLES.

Volume First, Arms of Great Britain. | Volume Second, Arms of Scotland.